CW00521560

Cricket in Wales, Volume 2

'LUCKY' JIM PLEASS

The Memoirs of Glamorgan's 1948 County Championship Winner

Andrew Hignell

To Alun,

Best wishes,

[signature]

ST DAVID'S PRESS

Cardiff

Published in Wales by St. David's Press, an imprint of
Ashley Drake Publishing Ltd
PO Box 733
Cardiff
CF14 7ZY
www.st-davids-press.com

First Impression – 2014

ISBN 978-1-902719-36-8
© Ashley Drake Publishing Ltd 2014
Text © Andrew Hignell 2014

British Library Cataloguing-in-Publication Data.
A CIP catalogue for this book is available from the British Library.

CONTENTS

"This book is dedicated to all of those people involved in the Normandy Landings during the summer of 1944"

FOREWORD

Cricket is a team game, and whilst some batsmen, bowlers or fielders will grab the headlines, it's often the contribution of other members of the eleven which has played a bigger part in victory. I know from my long career as an off-spinner with Glamorgan County Cricket Club that it was often the efforts of others in making a series of good stops in the field which helped to build up pressure on an opposition batsman, and although it was my name, or that of the catcher, which ultimately was recorded in the scorebook, it was the other members of the team who helped to hasten the fall of that particular wicket.

Sport, in general, is full of unsung heroes and people who are prepared to devote many long hours to the good of a team or a sporting organisation. Up and down the country, there are countless numbers of coaches and other volunteers who give up so much of their spare time, especially in developing the next generation of sportsmen and women, whilst there are ground staff, green-keepers and others who spend hour upon hour tending to the pitches, wickets or greens on which we play our sport. Add to this the many other support staff who look after, and tend, the equine and human bodies engaged in sporting activities throughout the year, and there is, in total, literally a cast of thousands without whom so much pleasure and satisfaction would be gained.

As far as Jim Pleass was concerned, he was one of these sportsmen whose time in the spotlight was all too brief, but without whom, so much collective success might not have been possible. Reading this fascinating book, I can but only admire Jim's contributions during Glamorgan's Championship-winning summer of 1948 or his efforts with the bat against the 1951 South Africans at Swansea, as well as at Harrogate against Yorkshire in 1955 in seeing the Welsh county to a couple of historic victories. Had he failed in each of these games, or not been so much of a livewire in the field under Wilf Wooller's captaincy,

Robert Croft

I can only wonder at how different the course of Glamorgan's cricketing history might have been.

But Jim was not only an unsung hero on the cricketing fields of Wales and England, he was also one of many thousands of people who heroically took part in the Normandy Landings of June 1944. As someone who has lived in peacetime and has never had to undertake National Service, I can only wonder what must have been going through Jim's mind as a young man in his late teens when he had to swap his sporting kit for military uniform and then in his early twenties undergo preparations ahead of D-Day, especially not knowing if he would return home alive, never mind play sport again.

My generation, like several others, therefore owes a huge debt of gratitude to the efforts of Jim and his comrades. As we as a nation in 2014 look back seventy years to events in northern France during that D-Day summer of 1944, as well as remembering a hundred years ago the start of the Great War in August 1914, we should never forget the sacrifices which so many others made so that we could enjoy our sport in peacetime.

ROBERT CROFT
Glamorgan and England
May 2014

INTRODUCTION

Jim Pleass is not a household name. Even within Glamorgan County Cricket Club, now splendidly housed at the SWALEC Stadium and basking in the honour of staging regular international cricket following the redevelopment of the Club's headquarters in the Welsh capital, there are only a small number who remember his name, or his time with Glamorgan – either as a player or as a committee member. Similarly, there are no stands or suites named in his honour. His is just one of many faces on the walls of the Club's plush pavilion where photographs hang of former Glamorgan teams as well as snapshots of the annual gatherings of the Club's Former Players Association.

Yet the man who was born in Cardiff in 1923 achieved something that only a handful of the five hundred or so people who have proudly worn the daffodil-sweater since the Club's formation in 1888, can claim to have also matched, winning, some sixty summers after the Club's creation, their first-ever County Championship title.

For Jim, the delight in being a member of Glamorgan's Championship-winning team in 1948 – the first to bring the county crown to Wales, and to the dismay of the London Press – came four years after he had faced a massive test of his own fortitude and strength of character, as the callow twenty-one year old was one of the many thousands of brave men on board the massive flotilla of vessels of all shapes and sizes which took part in the Normandy Landings of June 1944.

After the immense personal challenges he faced as a wireless operator on the landing crafts which headed across the English Channel on D-Day and it's aftermath on the bloody beach-heads of Northern France, it was with sheer joy and pride that four years later he went to battle on the cricket fields of Wales and England under the direction of the fearless Wilf Wooller – another man whose wartime experiences had shaped a steely character, and transformed a happy-go-lucky amateur into a hard-nosed and tough cricketer. Wooller was a stern and uncompromising leader on the field, never one to budge an inch in the name of Glamorgan CCC, yet off the field, you could not find a more charming and affable companion, always ready to buy a member of the opposition a drink at the end of the day's play and to chat away in a cordial fashion.

Indeed, it was under this particular Field Marshall that Jim – by nature a quiet and self-effacing character – blossomed and became an integral part of the first-ever Glamorgan team to win the County Championship. His sharp and alert fielding won rich praise from opposing teams, and allied to his steady batting, Jim remained in the Glamorgan side until the mid 1950s, by which time he had also achieved the notable distinction of scoring a maiden century as his side secured their first-ever victory on Yorkshire soil.

As a schoolboy before the War, Jim had watched Glamorgan play at Cardiff, Neath and Swansea and after seeing Glamorgan's match against the 1938 Australians, and being enraptured by their batting, he had a clear ambition, namely that one day he would play for the Welsh county. He duly achieved this in 1947 and the following year, he wrote his name into the Clubs annals.

But four years earlier, he had been very, very close to losing his life during D-Day as unbeknown to him, the landing craft he was manning was heading straight towards a German mine. Another, less fortunate, vessel steamed past but almost immediately after overtaking, it struck the mine towards which Jim and his colleagues had unwittingly been heading. Everyone on board the other vessel was killed instantly with Jim and his colleagues watching in horror as the fragments of the craft and its unfortunate occupants were strewn across the water. Lucky Jim indeed!

This book would not have been possible without the help of several former Glamorgan players including Peter Walker, Don Shepherd, Ossie Wheatley, Tony Lewis, Roger Davis and the late Wilf Wooller. My thanks also to the late John Billot and J.B.G. Thomas, plus Katrina Coopey of the Local Studies Dept. of Cardiff Library, David Herbert of Cardiff CC, Joan Pockett who helped to type up an early manuscript, as well as to Jim's son Brian who assisted with the final compilation of text. My thanks also to Richard Shepherd of Cardiff City FC and the late Roderick Suddaby of the Imperial War Museum for his advice on military matters and the D-Day landings. All of the photographs are from Jim's family album and the archives of Glamorgan CCC.

ANDREW HIGNELL
April 2014

1

EARLY DAYS IN CARDIFF

1923 was not a good summer for Glamorgan CCC. It was their third year as a first-class county, having been elevated from the ranks of the Minor County Championship in 1921, after a long campaign for recognition at a higher level. But by the end of July, the Welsh county had recorded just a solitary victory from their eighteen County Championship matches. Thirteen games had ended in defeat – four by the comprehensive margin of an innings and a further seven by either nine or ten wickets.

The summer of 1923 ended with Glamorgan finishing sixteenth out of seventeen teams in the Championship table, with only Northamptonshire below them despite the fact that the Welsh county had lost more games than their counterparts from the East Midlands. In all, a total of thirty-seven players appeared for Glamorgan in first-class games that summer, with some of the amateurs and professionals chosen by the well-meaning selectors struggling to make the step up to County Championship cricket.

John Hinwood, a capable player in club cricket, had the misfortune to bag a pair in his only first-class appearance whilst signings Fred Geary and Basil Rogers – who had apparently impressive records in club cricket in the Midlands – each proved to be somewhat below county standard and left the cash-strapped officials from Glamorgan rueing the fact that the Club's flimsy finances preventing them from hiring the services of more talented recruits. In fact, things were so bad that at the end of the summer, the captain Tom Whittington – who had done so much in securing first-class status in 1921 – resigned and left South Wales and left South Wales to take up a teaching post in Sussex.

With defeat following defeat, there had been mutterings about whether or not Glamorgan had been a worthy addition to the ranks of the first-class game. There seemed to be no discernable sign of headway either, and the Club had certainly not progressed from the previous year which had ended with them short of players for the closing match of the summer against Leicestershire at the Arms Park and with others injured on the eve of the game, the net result was that a fifteen schoolboy was hastily drafted in shortly before the start to make his one and only appearance in county cricket!

Infant Jim with his father

Teenager Jim with his father and uncle

A bashful Jim with his mother

A very young Jim!

In contrast, 1923 was a very good year for Edward and Eva Pleass, who lived in a terraced property in Cardiff's Splott Road, adjacent to the junction with South Park Road, as they celebrated the birth of their first son – James Edward. Splott was the neighbourhood where many of the Pleass family lived, with one uncle being a carpenter, another a wagon builder and a third a ship's clerk based in the dockland complex a mile or so away, close to the mouth of the River Taff.

Jim's parents had been fortunate to secure the house in Splott Road, next door to the Grovesnor Hotel, an imposing three-storey building and busy public house, which had been built during the 1890s when Splott was a prosperous inner suburb. For many decades, the Grosvenor's products quenched the thirsts of the local residents and dockland workers, and building acted as focal point for the local community.

I was born in what looked from the outside a quite imposing terraced property in Splott – an area which is now a poorer part of Cardiff, but back in the 1920s, and with some justification, it gave the impression of affluence, with many of the local residents being employed by the prosperous dockland.

Splott had developed in the closing decades of the late 19th century with Splott Road leading to the dockland complex of the River Taff, as well as being close to the East Moors steelworks which had been opened in 1890 by Guest Keen and Nettlefolds who owned the thriving Dowlais ironworks in Merthyr. Just around the corner form the Grosvenor was Splott Park, where through the liberality of landowner Lord Tredegar, a popular recreational area developed for the local community.

Although Wales, in common with the rest of Britain, was still recovering from the ravages of the Great War, the coal and shipping trade was flourishing at this time in the Cardiff area, and the adjacent steel works at East Moors was working to capacity.

The inside of our house was dark and somewhat forbidding, and yet, from just the other side of one brick wall came sounds of colourful chatter and revelry during the opening hours of the Grosvenor, with its bars full of animated dockworkers, steelworkers, and local tradesmen.

At the time, the popular means of transport into, out of, and around Splott, was the tramcar, which could be heard rumbling and screeching its raucous way from the city centre to the docks, and which passed around its final corner just a hundred yards away from my birthplace before making its ultimate run down to the dock gates.

I have very vague memories of the three years I spent in that environment and the only two matters of note were firstly that my Grandfather, not noticing me crawling along the hallway, contrived to trample on my head – an unfortunate accident and one which left me with a headache for some time and, so my friends told me,

Jim and his brothers in the back garden of their home in Fairwater

accounted for the odd quirks in my character! The other important event saw me, at the tender age of two and a half, being packed off to the local infant's school in Moorland Road, where I soon showed that there had been no lasting ill effects from this accident.

1926 saw the advent of the General Strike, but it also witnessed a change in circumstances for the Pleass family. My father, who worked for an insurance company, seized an opportunity to purchase a semi-detached house called Gebria in Llangynidr Road in Fairwater, a newly-developing outer suburb, several miles to the west of the city centre. It was a blissful change, away from the bricks and mortar of the congested and polluted inner city, and I can honestly say that growing up among the green fields, trees and swift-running streams of crystal-clear water was idyllic.

School for me meant a daily walk of two miles each way to receive mixed elementary education in the nearby village of St. Fagans, and a look at the old and faded copies of school reports indicate that I was keen and adept in assimilating such of the three "R's" as were being imparted. I hasten to add that one of the chief reasons I did well at school was the sudden realisation that nothing in this world was as important as to be able to participate in sport, and in particular, the only two games that I considered really existed – association football and cricket.

2

LEARNING CRICKET AND FOOTBALL

1927 was a great year in the history of sport in Cardiff with the city's football team defeating Arsenal in the FA Cup Final at Wembley as the famous trophy left English soil for the first-ever time. Cardiff City FC had, in fact, begun life as Riverside Cricket Club, which like so many other amateur teams during the closing years of the 19th century, had based their activities in the public recreation ground at Sophia Gardens, close to the inner suburb of Riverside. The members of the cricket club so enjoyed themselves that in 1899 they decided to maintain their camaraderie and sporting friendships during the winter months by forming a football club. They soon joined the recently-formed Cardiff and District League before amalgamating with another local club – the Riverside Albions – in 1902/03 in order to join the South Wales Amateur League, and to participate in the various knock-out competitions which were sanctioned by the South Wales and Monmouthshire Football Association.

After much success in the League, the club's officials mounted a campaign for their team to be called Cardiff City, and also to become a professional club, and on September 5th, 1908, they got the backing of the South Wales and Monmouthshire Football Association. With an upswing in interest in professional football across South Wales, the next few years saw the club acquire, from the Bute Estate, a plot of land in Grangetown which they subsequently developed into their home ground, and the newly incorporated Cardiff City Association Football Club Limited played their inaugural professional match on September 1st, 1910 at Ninian Park against Aston Villa, then the First Division champions, and in front of a crowd of 7,000.

Having played with success in the Southern League before the Great War, Cardiff City spent one further season in the Southern League as football resumed following the cessation of hostilities, before being invited to join the Football League Second Division for the 1920/21 season. They were acknowledged as the strongest team in Wales and on August 30th, 1920, around 25,000 people were present at Ninian Park to watch their inaugural Football League match with Clapton Orient.

Unlike the travails and regular reversals encountered by Glamorgan CCC, Cardiff City FC met with great success playing at this higher level, and they were promoted to the top flight of English Football at the first attempt. It came at the end of a season which had seen them enjoy a great run in the FA Cup, reaching the semi-final stage, where they lost to Wolverhampton Wanderers after a replay. Moreover, their gates rose to an average of 29,000 – a very far cry from the thousand of so die-hard cricket supporters who regularly watched Glamorgan play at Cardiff Arms Park or St. Helen's, Swansea.

The 1920s duly proved to be a golden decade for the football club, with the 1923/24 season proving to be one of their best-ever in the League. A dramatic season saw Cardiff City and Huddersfield Town tussle for the title, and after a dramatic final day when their top scorer Len Davies missed a vital penalty, goal average meant that the Welsh club had to settle for second place. The players were not disheartened as the following year they reached the final of the FA Cup. 1924/25 proved to be as dramatic as the year before with Welsh international Willie Davies scoring directly from a corner with the last kick of the quarter-final to set up a semi-final tie with Blackburn Rovers. Cardiff City duly won this game 3-1 and met Sheffield United at Wembley. It proved to be a dour final, played out in front of 91,763 fans, with England international Fred Tunstall scoring the only goal of the contest which saw the Cup head north to Yorkshire.

Two years later the Cup headed to Wales as Cardiff City made up for a fairly miserable time in the League and *en route* to Wembley they defeated, amongst others, Aston Villa, Bolton Wanderers, Reading and Chelsea, with the latter being beaten in a home replay after a goalless draw at Stamford Bridge in front of a crowd of 70,184.

St. George's Day 1927 saw massive queues of people boarding trains at Cardiff's mainline railway station as April 23rd went down in Welsh sporting folklore when Fred Keenor's team lifted the cup, defeating Arsenal thanks to a goal in the 74th minute when Hughie Ferguson collected a throw from the right by George MacLachlan, before hurrying a tame shot toward the Arsenal goal. Dan Lewis, the Arsenal goalkeeper, appeared to safely collect the ball but, under pressure from the advancing Len Davies, he rather clumsily allowed the ball to roll through his grasp. In a desperate attempt to retrieve the ball, Lewis only succeeded in knocking the ball with his elbow backwards into his own net.

As well as being the first time the Cup had been taken out of England, the 1927 final was also the first to be broadcast by BBC Radio, and for those Cardiffians unable to travel to London, they could listen to the exploits of the Bluebirds and share in the delight of Fred Keenor who received the trophy from King George V only seven years after the Club had first entered the Football League.

With Cardiff awash with football fever, it was no surprise that Jim should take an interest in sport and after hearing about how Cardiff won the FA Cup, it was understandable that he developed an early ambition to be a soccer goalkeeper.

From the age of five or six upwards I became obsessed by the desire to excel at cricket and football. Every spare moment would be taken up at home either kicking a ball, or belting it against a wall in our garden with the aid of an old, over-oiled bat, which I had found deep in the recesses of the cricket bag belonging to my Uncle, Bill Pritchard. He had been a handy player in his own right with Cardiff Cricket Club, although the First World War had interrupted his playing career. By the 1920s he had taken up umpiring and Uncle Bill was only too delighted to see me enjoy hitting a tennis ball with his old bat in the small back garden of our home in Fairwater.

The FA Cup comes to Wales!

Soccer, too, was not far behind in prominence in my attentions, and my early ambitions were to become a goalkeeper with a first division football team. However, these were somewhat thwarted by my inability to grow beyond 5 feet 6 inches, and also by an opposing centre-forward who in a school match contrived to relieve me of two front teeth when I bravely – and foolishly – hurled myself at his feet in an effort to capture the ball.

During the mid 1930s, we moved house again, but our new home – a spanking new semi-

Members of the successful Cardiff City team that won the 1927 FA Cup

A photo taken at Jim's 7th birthday party, in 1930

detached property was only a stones' throw away from the existing one and situated in a rather exclusive, tree-lined close known as The Drive in Fairwater which had previously been the avenue leading towards a large, country mansion.

Our move from Gebria in Llangynidr Road to number 6 The Drive followed the promotion of my father to Branch Manager of the British General Insurance Company Limited. By this time, I had also done quite well for myself having gained a place at Canton High School, a large, modern secondary school where I had plenty of opportunity to play cricket on a more competitive basis and with vastly improved facilities. Through Uncle Bill's encouragement, I had played a few games for the boy's team at the St. Fagans club, which was a mile or so's walk away from my new home. I didn't mind, though, walking through the fields out, and back, to the St. Fagans ground in Croft-y-gennau Road, especially as it gave me an opportunity to play my summer sport.

I didn't really receive any coaching as such, either at the St. Fagans club or at Canton High School. Instead, I was just encouraged to play by the enthusiastic school teachers and the other adults at St. Fagans. There was probably the odd tip about field placing and where to hit the ball, but I'd probably picked up most of the rudiments about batting and hitting the ball with Uncle Bill's bat in the back garden at home. This combination of practice and apparent natural talent soon led to better things at Canton as I secured a place in the school's 1st XI when still only twelve years

The Canton High School cricket team of the late 1930s with Jim sat on the ground, front right

old, and my earliest games for the team were playing with, and against, eighteen-year-olds.

My batting for Canton High school also attracted the attention of some of the officials of Cardiff CC who oversaw the Cardiff Schoolboys team which played matches at weekends in school term and at various times during the summer holidays against boy's teams from other places in South Wales as well as touring teams. No doubt, Uncle Bill also put in a good word for me and despite being one of the youngest,

The Canton High School rugby team of 1938. Jim is standing second from the right in the front row.

and smallest in the squad, I played in a few games for the Cardiff Schoolboys team.

There was one downside however as far as sport was concerned by attending Canton. During the winter it was only rugby which was played, and the playing of soccer was frowned upon by my teachers. Despite my short stature and frame, I managed to make the school team, largely because I was a quick runner and, as a winger, I could think on my feet about which way to swerve or run around an opponent. But, when facing much larger opponents, it was more about self-preservation than rugby-playing skill, and despite being on the receiving end of some thumping tackles, playing rugby was quite good fun, but from my own point of view, it was nothing at all like football which remained my favourite winter pastime.

Quite a few of my friends at school, as well as several of the lads who lived near me in the Fairwater area also loved football, and avidly followed the fortunes of Cardiff City and the big English clubs. Starved of the opportunity to play the game at school, we formed our own football team and played several matches in the fields near our homes at weekends or after school against other junior teams of like-minded and equally enthusiastic souls.

In my early 'teens it occasionally crossed my mind that in the attractive bungalow adjoining our house, there were

The Fairwater boys football team of 1932-33 with Jim crouching forward, back left.

other attractions in the shapes (and what shapes!) of two auburn-haired sisters, who were possessed of vivacious personalities and charm in addition to their physical attributes. However, despite these potential diversions, I focussed my main desires on sport, playing cricket in the summer and football in the winter.

As the 1930s unfolded, my sporting education progressed, much I may add, to the detriment of my academic education especially in those subjects which schoolmasters believe to be essential to the well-being and future prosperity of their pupils. Why on earth they were obliged to introduce homework as well was quite beyond me!

My homework would invariably be done in the spring and summer with a minimum of time and effort, in order to make way for the really important matters that lay ahead – namely the playing of a Test Match between England and Australia at the side of the house, with the shed door suitably marked up in chalk as a wicket, and an equally-eager companion to act as the opposition. What contests they were, often lasting for hours and hours on end. My word, how tolerant my parents must have been!

The proud Headmaster of Canton High School sits with his cricket team of 1939. Jim is sitting next to him on the right.

3

A FIRST ENCOUNTER WITH BRADMAN

The fortunes of Glamorgan County Cricket Club improved significantly during the 1930s after a series of very difficult years in the 1920s. There were times when the Welsh county could have folded, and in the early 1930s the effects of the Great Depression – plus a series of summers with little success – prompted the Club's committee to discuss whether or not they could continue as a first-class side.

By this time, Maurice Turnbull, the son of a Cardiff shipping-magnate was at the helm and the gifted batsman was unwavering in his opinion that Glamorgan CCC should continue. He had the rock-solid support of Johnnie Clay, the off-spinner from Monmouthshire whose own county career had begun in the 1920s as a fast bowler. Both shared the dream, held by the other romantics who had been instrumental in Glamorgan's elevation into the County Championship in 1921, and in the course of the next few years, Maurice and Johnnie did everything in their powers to consolidate the fortunes of Glamorgan CCC and to promote the Club as Wales' representative in the first-class game.

In particular, Maurice and Johnnie had a wide network of friends and associates, especially in Cardiff Docks, who they could lean upon for financial support and during 1932 and 1933 they spent countless hours attending fund-raising events, besides searching for new talent who could wear the Glamorgan daffodil with pride. Glamorgan CCC was not alone as the early 1930s were difficult years for cricket professionals all over the UK as the effects of the economic slump hit clubs and other sporting organizations, and affected the monetary terms offered to the players. But Maurice and Johnnie had a trump card in that Glamorgan was the only Welsh-based county paying at that level, and by the spring of 1933 there were pledges of sufficient support for the committee to agree to carry on.

The 1930s also witnessed an important change in the identity of Glamorgan CCC as under the inspirational leadership of Maurice Turnbull, the Club developed a sharper and more obvious Welsh identity with home-grown youngsters given their chance, largely in the belief that they could do no worse than the has-beens or nearly-beens which Glamorgan had signed

Jim, in his cricket whites, in the garden of his home in Fairwater.

during the 1920s. Bill Hitch, the former England and Surrey seam bowler, was also signed as Club coach and during the 1930s he helped to identify and nurture new talent.

An important development came during 1934 when Monmouthshire's officials approached Glamorgan and suggested a merger. Monmouthshire had been playing in the Minor County Championship since 1901, but their finances were in a dire state and they could not continue on their own. Consequently, they suggested merging with Glamorgan who could field a 2nd XI in the Minor County competition, thereby also drawing on the pool of talent in the neighbouring county. The Glamorgan committee agreed, and 1935 saw a strengthening in the Club's resources as a number of promising youngsters were blooded in the Minor County competition before making their debut in the 1st XI.

The net result was that by the late 1930s the cricketing infrastructure across South Wales was in a far better position than ten years before. Programmes and strategies were put in place to identify and nurture home-grown talent, and as far as Jim was concerned, he was one of the first crop of promising young batsmen in the Cardiff area to benefit from the improved practice facilities at the Arms Park. Having shone at Canton High School and for the Cardiff Schoolboys team, he was invited to play for Cardiff Cricket Club and in 1939 – at the age of just sixteen – he made his debut for their 1st XI.

His cricketing ambitions had also been strengthened by watching county cricket at the Arms Park after Uncle Bill – who had also taken Jim to watch Cardiff City play at Ninian Park – invited Jim and some of his young friends from Fairwater to watch Glamorgan in their County Championship games.

I had enjoyed my visits to Ninian Park with Uncle Bill but I was really thrilled to get an opportunity to watch the Glamorgan team play at the Arms Park, especially as I had heard some of the Cardiff cricketers talk about the various people who represented Glamorgan either as an amateur or a professional. This chatter in the Cardiff dressing room gave me a sort of link with the people who I duly saw proudly wear the daffodil sweater, and this sense of association with the county players – albeit quite tenuous – helped to further fuel my cricketing ambitions.

As I had no desire to be a bowler, it was the Glamorgan batsmen who became my earliest cricketing heroes. In particular, I was hugely impressed by the fluent strokeplay of captain Maurice Turnbull and the sublime way, without fuss or an extra show of bravado, he managed to dominate visiting bowlers and score runs all around the wicket.

Cyril Stuart

Cyril Smart was another favourite of mine, especially for the way he used to thump balls into the flats lining the Westgate Street boundary. Whenever talking about him to my young friends at the Cardiff club, I was told about the way a few years before the building of these flats, Cyril had nonchalantly

An aerial view of the Arms Park ground in Cardiff during the early 1930s.

Emrys Davies and Arnold Dyson going out to bat for Glamorgan in May 1946.

swatted balls across the road and into the foyer, or through the plate-glass windows of the hotels on the far-side of the street!

Emrys Davies also impressed me with his technically correct strokeplay, immaculately straight bat and unflappable attitude. After accepting the offer to bat up the order for various Cardiff teams, I often imagined myself as Emrys facing the quicks on the county circuit and stoutly fending off the bowlers, little believing that one day I would have the great fortune of walking onto the pitch alongside him to represent Glamorgan.

During the late 1930s my cricket-loving uncle also took me to watch Glamorgan play at Ynysangharad Park in Pontypridd as well as further west to Swansea where I was able to sit amongst the hundreds of spectators and immerse myself in the games at the delightful ground overlooking Swansea Bay. I was fortunate enough in 1938 to be there, with thousands of others, when the great Don Bradman played again at Swansea.

July 30th 1938 saw the Australians and the legendary batsman Don Bradman, who was making his third visit to the UK, travel to Swansea to meet Maurice Turnbull and the Glamorgan side. A couple of days before their arrival there was excited chatter in the towns across South Wales about the likely make-up of the Australian side, so there were broad smiles all over the region when news finally filtered through that the Don was in the tourist's line-up, giving the sports-mad population a chance to see the man whose very presence at the crease, and exceptional batting talents, had prompted the `Bodyline` furore on the England tour to Australia in 1932/33 which nearly saw the countries cut off diplomatic relations with each other.

The Glamorgan side of 1938 was far stronger than any the Welsh county had previously fielded against touring teams, with both Turnbull and Clay having played at the highest level for England. In particular, Clay was also at the height of his powers, having taken a Club record 176 wickets the previous summer, and having the deserved reputation as being one of the best off-spinners on the county circuit. The prospect of watching Bradman bat against Clay was a mouth-watering one, and with a full house likely at the St. Helen's ground, the Glamorgan Treasurer was already rubbing his hands in glee at the prospect of a bumper gate to further swell the club's coffers.

But the weather played a hand, as the first two days of the game were badly affected by rain, and it was only on the third morning that the crowd got their wish as out walked the great man in his baggy green cap. Thinking of Glamorgan's finances, Turnbull had gathered his bowlers around him and said "Don't try and get Bradman out too quickly, as there are still a few places in the crowd." Dutifully, Clay followed these instructions, as news that `The Don` was at the crease quickly spread around the town, and scores of people headed for St. Helen's – some no doubt with the flimsiest of excuses for leaving work!

Within fifteen minutes or so, of Bradman arriving at the crease, there was barely a spare seat on the ground, and with the crowd now standing over a dozen deep around the boundary edge, Turnbull had a quick word with Clay and told the off-spinner that it was alright for him to try and dismiss Bradman. It didn't take Clay very long either as Bradman – like so many other batsmen before and after on the county circuit – was lured down the track by Johnnie's subtle bowling and smartly stumped by wicket-keeper Haydn Davies for 17. The Australian maestro departed somewhat crestfallen, but the crowd were happy as they had seen the great man bat, albeit very briefly, whilst the Glamorgan Treasurer was equally pleased as he sat in the pavilion, counting the enormous pile of coins from the gate receipts.

Sat in the crowd at the St. Helen's ground was an enraptured Jim Pleass. He had seen Bradman in the flesh and, for a while, he had also watched the Australian maestro with bat in hand:

The bad weather had prevented us from travelling on the first couple of days, so I was pleased at last to travel to Swansea with my uncle and several others from the

Don Bradman (left) walks out for the toss with Glamorgan captain Maurice Turnbull at Swansea in 1938.

Cardiff club. We had left Cardiff early in the morning and we arrived in Swansea a couple of hours or so before play was due to start. We thought that it would be straightforward to get tickets on the day, so you can imagine our surprise when we arrived to find the St. Helen's ground almost encircled by people, all desperate – just like us – to watch Bradman bat against Glamorgan.

My uncle knew a few people and I'm not sure if he pulled a few strings or not, but we were able to get in. To be honest, I don't remember much about Bradman batting and most of my memories from that day revolve around the journey down to Swansea and being surrounded by so many cricket-loving people. The atmosphere at Swansea certainly left it's mark on me, and reinforced my dream of one-day playing for Glamorgan. Little did I think that I would later get a chance to play for the Welsh county against Bradman.

4

WAR SERVICE

1939 had seen Jim Pleass play his first match for Cardiff's 1st XI. The summer also saw Maurice Turnbull play his last game for his beloved county, with his final appearance for Glamorgan coming in August 1939 at a time when the clouds of War had firmly fixed themselves over Europe.

There had been a rather unreal atmosphere to sporting events in 1939, as Jim together with the other youngsters from the Cardiff club gathered on a regular basis at the nets at the Arms Park for coaching sessions and the occasional practice session with county coach Bill Hitch. 1938 had seen the actions of one man at the centre of the conversation amongst the youngsters at Cardiff's nets as the chatter focussed on the astonishing batting feats of Don Bradman. A year on, it was the deeds of another man which took centre-stage as the youngsters tried to put talk of Adolf Hitler, and an imminent War with Germany, out of their minds and to focus instead on the upcoming fixtures.

Once again, Jim took the opportunity to watch some county cricket in 1939 and like others across South Wales he was delighted when it was confirmed by the MCC selectors that Emrys Davies, the stalwart all-rounder had been chosen in the party for the winter tour to India in 1939/40. Jim was delighted for his batting idol, who had already featured in the England team which he had chosen for the imaginary Test Matches with his friends at Fairwater! Now it looked as if these dreams would become reality with the yeoman all-rounder poised to appear in an England sweater on the sub-continent. But in August confirmation came through from Lord's that in light of the German invasion of Poland and the deteriorating international situation, the MCC winter tour to India had been cancelled, and any thoughts Jim had of proudly writing DE Davies, Glamorgan and England, in his autograph book had to be put on hold.

Glamorgan's last home game of 1939 saw them beaten inside two days, against Surrey at Swansea on a wicket giving considerable help to the bowlers, and with the newspapers full of doom and gloom, they could be easily excused for having their minds on other things. Indeed, the final match of the season was away to Leicestershire, and there was little cricket chat amongst

The Cardiff schoolboys team of 1939 with Jim sat front right

the amateurs and professionals as they headed off to the Aylestone Road ground knowing that War had been declared on Germany.

Johnnie Clay was unavailable for selection as events at Cardiff Docks where he worked necessitated his remaining in South Wales, with defences being erected and gun implacements completed. With the nation on a war-footing, it was a measure of Maurice Turnbull's mental resilience that he banished the gloomy thoughts about the War with a sparkling innings of 156. Indeed, it was a case of business as usual for the Glamorgan skipper as he struck 2 sixes and 18 fours in an innings which saw Glamorgan achieve a first innings lead. An early evening thunderstorm then all but flooded the ground, and on the final day, play did not commence until mid-afternoon. There was not enough time remaining even for the inspirational Glamorgan captain to devise a winning strategy, so with a positive outcome out of the question, it was a case of Glamorgan batting out time.

Maurice generously dropped down the order to give others a chance to bat, and in the final few overs before the close, the loss of Glamorgan's seventh wicket finally brought Turnbull to the crease. The Glamorgan skipper was unbeaten on

Jim receives an award at a Cardiff CC dinner.

nought when umpires Lee and Elliott called time and drew the stumps. There were many handshakes all round as the players departed for the pavilion, with everyone hoping that they would soon be back playing cricket again, and as Maurice unbuckled his pads, none of his colleagues could dare to imagine that the wonderful Glamorgan skipper had played his final innings for the club for whom he had done so much.

Cardiff CC 1940 - Jim is second left in the back row.

For Jim, the summer of 1939 drew to a close with further matches for Cardiff's 1st XI, plus an invite to attend some of Glamorgan's winter coaching sessions at the Arms Park. With the county club running a 2nd XI in the Minor County Championship as well as a Colts side, their coaches had provisionally organised a series of coaching sessions in one of the corridors of the North Stand at the Arms Park where they could run their eye over some of the promising youngsters who might win a place in the

The Cardiff Corries football team of 1940, with Jim third right sitting in the front row.

Colts team. Jim had impressed for the Cardiff club, in addition to being captain of the Canton High School side, but with everyone's mind on far weightier matters, Jim knew that the Glamorgan officials were only going through the motions and that the War was likely to prevent these practices from taking place.

Jim had also impressed the talent scouts of Cardiff City FC, and his excellent play on the wing for both Canton High School and the Cardiff Corinthians team had led to an approach by the City club to take part in various trial games at Ninian Park. Indeed, officials had also outlined to Jim how much he might earn as a professional if he were to decide to join the Club on leaving school.

1939 saw me poised to break into professional sport, and the prospect of being paid to play football in the winter, and possible the same for cricket, greatly appealed. I'd not had any careers advice and my only thoughts were really about playing sport as often as I could. The sums mentioned were not as great as the enormous ones which today's professionals earn, but even so, my head was buzzing with these numbers when I returned home to speak with my parents after the initial meeting with the management at Cardiff City. But my parents advice was that I should concentrate on finishing my education, but like everyone else, I had other things to think about in my last years at school as the Second World War got underway.

In common with many other youngsters, and following in the footsteps of my father, I joined the local Home Guard. My father had served in the trenches during the Great War and growing up, myself and my brothers had heard his quite harrowing

tales of gas, mud and depravity. Events in South Wales in 1939 were less grim and bloody, and I was only too pleased to do my stint of duty preparing for the likely invasion of German paratroopers, especially as it was not too unpleasant, walking a few miles to the village of St Fagans to do a couple of hours sentry duty outside the well-known Castle, and then spending the

The Canton High School rugby team of 1939-40 with Jim holding the shield which the team won after a successful season.

rest of the night learning the intricacies of Solo whilst in a card school dominated by seasoned veterans.

The summer of 1940 therefore saw me regularly walk across the fields to St.Fagans, retracing the steps I had made a few years before with my cricket kit, out to the Croft-y-Gennau ground. But there was very little sporting activity for me to get involved with that summer. In fact, the only exercise I got with the Home Guard was when we were supposed to crawl across muddy fields and attempt to capture an objective held by regular troops, who were probably as bored as we were by our efforts, and by a couple of German air raids, which saw a stick of bombs carving huge craters out of fields on the edge of the City, plus a few landmines which unfortunately dropped on residential areas.

One of the remarkable side-effects emanating from the activities of the German bombers was my success in gaining the coveted School Certificate in my last year at Canton High School. The need for obtaining some concrete evidence of my academic progress finally came home to me in that last year, and I did give some time and thought to the necessary revision. Even that had its pleasant moments, as I found the very attractive niece of a neighbour had similar problems, and we decided to share our time and resources, resulting in many hours in close proximity going through our notes and books whilst lying in the beautiful fields and woodland close to our home in Fairwater.

The major problem we faced was in trying to pass one of two compulsory subjects – Chemistry or Physics – and, as my marks in each subject rarely (if ever) were in excess of twenty out of a hundred the future looked ominous. It also happened that, at the very start of the chemistry exam, just after the papers had been handed out, an air raid warning sounded, and we were all packed off to the shelter area in the basement. When the all-clear sounded an hour later, and we resumed work in the classroom, it was amazing how much simpler the questions seemed, and my success was assured!

My delight at passing these exams and gaining the School Certificate was tempered by the fact that on leaving school, I now had to find a job. With football and cricket temporarily suspended, I had to banish my dreams of being a professional sportsman. I had no intention of following my father into the insurance profession, and, at first, I had the opportunity of becoming a clerk in a bank or work with a local firm which manufactured and laid asphalt surfaces for roads and roofs. I felt that the latter was a better proposition, especially as I would be outdoors so, in the Autumn of 1940, I took the plunge. The work was interesting, and somewhat educational, as I was able to spend a considerable time with the road gangs, who had their own fairly fixed ideas about life in general, and their lot in particular, plus a vocabulary that was limited, but which contained words and expressions the like of which I had never heard before.

After some months in this environment, I was taken under the wing of the boffins

Jim, in his military uniform, in 1941.

and subsequently spent time in the works laboratory, taking samples of the manufactured products; testing them; analysing them, and ensuring that they conformed with the accepted standards. As 1941 progressed, it became apparent that the War was escalating; that we weren't doing all that well, and that many of my colleagues were being called to the colours. Eventually, I decided that, if I had to join the forces, I would jump the gun by volunteering, which at least would mean that I could have some choice in the type of service I was prepared to give. It so happened that, in the Home Guard, I had been taught the Morse Code, and I was quite interested in it. As a result, I applied to join the Royal Corps of Signals, and sat back and waited for my call to arms.

The call, as usual, came at the most inopportune moment. I had been sent by the asphalt company, just after Christmas, to the far west of Wales to oversee a site project at an aerodrome in Pembrokeshire. I had not been there long when my parents telephoned to say that my papers had arrived, and that I was to report to a place called Catterick. As far as I was concerned, it could have been anywhere, but it turned out to be in North Yorkshire. A hurried journey back to Cardiff; some feverish packing and I was soon at the railway station at the crack of dawn, saying my farewells to the family, and waiting with some trepidation for the arrival of the Northern Express.

In the late afternoon, I was to be found sitting in a carriage on the last lap from Darlington to Richmond, with another lost-looking individual from Nottingham who was also bound on the same errand, plus a kindly middle-aged railway employee who gave us his home address in Darlington, and offered us his hospitality any weekend we were allowed to leave the Army camp if we so wished. In the ensuing months my new-found friend and I were to take full advantage of the kind offer, and that tiny terrace house in a Darlington suburb was like an oasis in the desert. We were always made welcome; shared meals and the warmth of the hearth with the family, and it was always a wrench to leave the fireside and return to the inhospitable camp.

5

MILITARY TRAINING

Like other sports-mad schoolboys, Jim had dreamt that his earliest days on leaving school life would be taken up with plenty of sporting activity. But like others of his generation, the early 1940s saw the nation's young bloods facing very different and more severe challenges to those posed on a sports field.

In particular, the major challenge was the next phase of the War. Following the retreat from Dunkirk in May and June 1940, and the subsequent Nazi occupation of France, Belgium and the Low Countries, it was clear that the next element would either see a German invasion of Britain, or an Allied Invasion somewhere in north-west Europe. As far as an Allied attack was concerned, wireless operators would play a vital role in these manoeuvres, either at the War Office in London or on the frontline, so 1942 and 1943 therefore saw Jim and his colleagues in the Royal Corps of Signals become involved in a host of activities and training exercises as they prepared for the Invasion.

The signal training was quite hard. Not only did we have to learn the intricacies of operating and maintaining the radio set, but we also had to be soldiers as well, and many were the hours spent in square-bashing, weapon training, and the like. Discipline was strict, as it had to be, and it mattered not that I had achieved a Morse sending rate of twelve words per minute in the Home Guard. In the Army I was expected to start again from scratch and do it the way they wanted it done.

In the months that passed there were few compensations, but I was fortunate enough to be able to display my ability at soccer, and it led to an invitation to play for the Army team against Doncaster Rovers' League side. At the very least, it meant getting away from the camp at Catterick for a couple of days, and it was well worth it even though we lost the match by five goals to one.

With initial training completed, thoughts began to turn to the future, and many were the rosy dreams of doing shift work in front of sophisticated radio equipment at, perhaps, the War Office, and alongside a pretty operative of the Women's Forces. Posting notices were eagerly scanned, but for me the dream of being in London swiftly faded; I was assigned to a newly-formed armoured division in the South of England at Slough.

Jim, at the Catterick military camp in 1942, sitting on the grass, third from the right.

The division occupied primitive wooden huts on the outskirts of the Berkshire town, and in the depths of the winter of 1942/43, it was quite unpleasant to stumble out from a reasonably warm hut in pitch-black and freezing conditions to take part in the inevitable roll-call, and afterwards to cross an open field to the ablutions hut, where one was expected to shave and wash in a trickle of cold water – that is, when it wasn't frozen solid.

Numerous night exercises were held, and if anyone can think of a worse way of spending cold winter nights than sitting in the back of an unheated canvas-covered truck with earphones on, trying to pick up a Morse signal of uncertain strength on a frequency being used by perhaps a dozen other stations, it would be most surprising.

When on the move, the wireless operator's job would be to lead the convoy in the signal truck, directing the driver by torch and map, with no signposts or place names available to assist. My claim to fame was pressed by misreading a map reference, and thus leading a long line of tanks, other armoured vehicles and supply trucks off the highway, through a gap in a hedge into a large and muddy field. The sight of a mobile column travelling round and round in circles in a desperate effort to find the road again on a night as black as ink, and with no lights allowed, is one I will never forget. Needless to say, it marked the end of my pathfinder duties!

By the summer of 1943, plans were in an advanced and top secret stage for what became known as the Normandy Landings. Under what was known as Operation Bodyguard, the Allies had instigated a comprehensive and complex series of deceptions which subsequently led to the landings on the beaches in Normandy achieving strategic and tactical surprise.

A key element behind the success of these operations was Operation Fortitude South which convinced Adolf Hitler and the German commanders that the Allies were planning a main attack across the Straits of Dover by the fictitious First United States Army Group led by George S. Patton. Jim and his colleagues were therefore involved in a series of training exercises in a variety of locations in Southern and Eastern England, using all kinds of landing craft.

From Yorkshire we moved to an isolated lakeside site in the flat wastes of East Anglia, where the highly secret units of the division, being inflatable amphibious tanks, could be put through their paces. There were unfortunate accidents at times, the worst being when, in the very centre of the deep lake, the tank driver inadvertently pulled the lever which deflated the cushion of air (the fore-runner of the Hovercraft), causing the tank and its occupants to sink like stones to the bottom, with no hope of rescue.

Just when it seemed as if I should be in the forefront of the impending invasion of France, fate decided to play it's little trick again. A Morse instructor in the Signals Training Unit in Huddersfield went permanently sick and I was given promotion to N.C.O and posted to take his place. It was quite a change in circumstances, as the new billet turned out to be a huge, substantially built woollen mill, six stories high. It was solid; it was dark and forbidding but comfortable, and it housed six hundred soldiers. One of the more intriguing duties I found as Orderly N.C.O on my particular floor was to ensure that, at 6am, the 150 or so occupants of the triple bunk beds were awakened and removed therefrom in the shortest possible time.

This pleasant sinecure, with attendant compensations of the occasional evening and weekend passes to view the attractions of the town, was too good to last. Late in 1943 came the news that the Unit was being disbanded. Once again, thoughts of a cosy War Office posting came to mind, but again fate played it's little joke. I was to travel to the West Coast of Scotland, where the newly-formed Combined Operations (Army, Navy and Air Force) Command were quartered in a naval base called H.M.S Dundonald, practising amphibious landings.

One redeeming feature of attachment to the Navy was that the food was a vast improvement on Army fare, although, after a few hours in small landing craft on the turbulent waters between the coast at Ayr and the Isle of Arran, food tended to be furthermost from one's thoughts. Needless to say, this build-up of forces and the concentrated training it involved meant that sporting interests were of no consequence; the nearest activity on the sporting front proved to be road-walking; not a route march as such, but a late night hike of nine miles back to base, having, after an evening out, courteously taken the current female friend home, and missing the last bus!

Another evening of note occurred when, while an in-patient at the local hospital recovering from a minor cyst operation, I became friendly with one of the attendant nurses. Having made an arrangement to meet her on her evening off, I contrived to struggle from my pyjamas into uniform surreptitiously after lights out; scrambled out of a window, down a drainpipe, and reversed the process after a pleasant few hours in her company.

Shortly after these exertions I was discharged from hospital and returned to camp, where our training was soon completed. The war for us was coming nearer, and a couple of us were duly posted south to Southampton, where we joined the complement of crew on a small, flat-bottomed landing craft for the purpose of manning the ship-to-shore radios in conjunction with our naval counterparts. L.C.H. 100 was to become our floating home for the next three months, most of the time being spent exercising and testing equipment in the Solent. When in harbour, we tied up alongside numerous similar craft, and, during the approaches to "D-Day", Southampton water was a veritable armada of ships as far as the eye could see.

6

NORMANDY LANDINGS

By the Spring of 1944 Allied commanders were still trying to convince Hitler that their plan was for a main attack across the Straits of Dover with the Normandy landings merely being a diversionary tactic. In fact on D-Day itself the deception was maintained by heavy bombers as part of Operations Glimmer and Taxable flying in highly precise patterns over the Straits of Dover, dropping radar-reflecting aluminium strips which created a picture on German radar of an invasion fleet moving across the straits, precisely at the same time as the "real" invasion fleet was heading to Normandy.

As far as the Normandy Invasion was concerned, the summer months of 1944 were the most favourable time, but only ten days each month were suitable for launching the operation with a day near the full Moon required both for illumination during the hours of darkness and helping to illuminate navigational landmarks for the crews of aircraft, gliders and landing craft and also a day with a spring tide, in order to provide the deepest possible water to help safe navigation over the defensive obstacles which had been placed by the German forces on the seaward approaches to the Normandy beaches.

With a full moon scheduled, Allied Expeditionary Force Supreme Commander Dwight D. Eisenhower selected June 5th as the date for the Invasion, but the weather which had been fine for most of May then deteriorated in early June, and with conditions unsuitable for a landing, with wind, high seas and low cloud, everything was put on hold. The Allied troop convoys, which were already at sea, were forced to take shelter in bays and inlets along the south coast of Britain for the night and await further instruction.

For a while, it looked as if after months and months of meticulous planning and cunning deception, everything would have to be cancelled, with the troops returning to their embarkation camps just a few hours after setting off for Northern France. But Eisenhower's chief meteorologist forecasted a brief improvement in conditions, and after much discussion by the various military personnel, Eisenhower ordered the invasion to proceed on June 6th. The Germans meanwhile took comfort from the existing poor conditions, which were much worse over Northern France than over the English Channel itself. Believing that no invasion would be possible for several days, some troops were stood down, whilst many senior officers went away for the weekend, with Field Marshal Erwin Rommel also taking a few days' leave to celebrate his wife's birthday.

D-Day duly took place on Tuesday, June 6th 1944, with an airborne assault landing of 24,000 British, American, Canadian and Free French airborne troops shortly after midnight, and an amphibious landing of Allied infantry and armoured divisions on the coast of France starting at 6:30 am. The operation proved to be the largest amphibious invasion in world history and was executed by land, sea and air under direct British command involving 73,000 Americans, 61,715 British and 21,400 Canadians, with landings taking place along a fifty-mile stretch of the Normandy coast divided into five sectors: Utah, Omaha, Gold, Juno, and Sword.

Amongst those heading to Gold Beach that fateful day was 21 year-old Jim Pleass.

On the 21st May, I had celebrated my 21st birthday. With the Invasion soon to happen, no shore leave was generally being allowed, but on occasions, special passes were issued and myself and a small group were fortunate to acquire these and spend a short time outside the dock precincts. Prior to that, however, the morning call of "up spirits" took place, during which the standard birthday practice of "sippers" was employed. This involved all and sundry leaving a drop of two of rum in their containers; pooling it and inviting me to quaff the lot. The next conscious moment came very much later, when I realised that, somehow, I had found my way into a large cinema in the centre of Southampton, and was being pulled upright by my colleagues while the National Anthem was played at the end of the evening performance!

This was the last bit of jollity for many, many weeks as a few days later, a "top brass" visit from General Eisenhower and Winston Churchill clearly indicated that the day of the invasion was rapidly approaching and on June 4th we duly cast off, moved down Southampton Water, turned to starboard at the Solent, and after midnight headed off in the general direction towards France, still not knowing precisely where we were heading.

As the day progressed, the wind freshened and the sea became spiteful. I went on deck after a spell in the wireless room, and was horrified to find that there was no other ship in sight – were we the only ones going, I thought to myself? It soon transpired that all ships had been recalled in view of the conditions, and, thankfully we duly made our way back into sheltered waters, anchoring alongside hundreds of other vessels. Twenty four hours later, it was "on" again, despite the weather having scarcely improved , and off we went in the blackness of night, pitching and rolling

One of the landing craft used on D Day.

so badly that most of us were too concerned with "mal de mer" to worry about what lay in front of us.

What was in front of us, and, indeed all around us swiftly became evident at dawn on that never-to-be-forgotten day – June 6th 1944. We had arrived at a point a hundred yards off-shore from the Normandy coast at Arromanches, or Gold Beach as it was designated in the D-Day, or Operation Overlord Plans. The grey sky was lit up by the flashes of rockets, plus shells of all sizes, and what seemed like hundreds of flares. The sea was scarcely to be seen, covered as it was by a vast array of ships, some of them firing at coastal targets, and others disgorging an army of men into smaller craft which hurriedly made for shore to lower their ramps and remove their human cargo. Enemy activity consisted of the few remaining strongpoints firing their "88's" at the fleet, but doing little damage before they were eliminated.

Once the beachhead was established, our job was to link beach signallers with the heavily armed cruisers and the like, directing their fire at pin-pointed targets. Within forty eight hours all was secure, and our work was done. For the next few

Arromanches

days, we patrolled the area just off the beaches, and the only real danger came from mines dropped by German planes at night, which did cause some damage.

In fact, the nearest wartime escape for me came the morning after one of these night drops. When not on radio duty, my supplementary task was to man the forward Oerlikon Anti-aircraft Gun, which was situated in the bows of the vessel. On this occasion, I was so placed, watching the bows as we cleaved through the water. A small landing craft personnel, carrying a group of senior officers, sped past us on our starboard side, swiftly cutting across our bows after passing in front of us but then promptly hit a mine and disintegrated into nothing. Had it not been for the landing craft going in front of us, we would have reached this point within another minute. The only evidence of the disaster was a motley collection of ripped clothing and headgear floating on the surface. There, but for the grace of God indeed.

It was about ten days after the initial onslaught that someone somewhere ordained that we had achieved personally all that we were likely to, and that it was high time that we were returned to our Scottish base to prepare for the next invasion, which was scheduled for the South of France. It proved, however, much more difficult to return to the U.K. than it had been to reach France in the first instance!

The initial vessel going back to the UK accepted us on board but then wound a mooring rope around its propellers, rendering itself hors de combat. Eventually, we found that the destroyer "Fury" was making the trip back and we managed to get on board. It proved though to be a most uncomfortable night for two reasons – firstly, we had to endure an anti-submarine attack which involved the dropping of depth charges far too near the stern as far as we were concerned, the effect being similar to experiencing an earthquake in the middle of a thunderstorm. Next came an attack of a different sort – the ship had recently been on duty in much warmer climes, and had acquired an indeterminate number of additional "passengers" about one inch long, which made their homes in the bulkheads. We had bedded down on top on the mess tables and, with every shake and shudder of the vessel, a dozen or more cockroaches duly tumbled down on us!

The next morning, coming in to the harbour at Portsmouth, more than made up for our sufferings, as it produced a marvellous feeling of euphoria at being back in our homeland after embarking on a journey which could have been our last, but which had only lasted two weeks. Our motley group of half a dozen Army signallers looked extremely scruffy, and with no kit to speak of, we thought we were back home. Well, nearly! A small boat was hailed, as the destroyer was anchoring in mid-stream, there being no available berth for her, and we were transferred. Unfortunately, the boat was not going to the dockside itself, so it was thought best to deposit us at the foot of a ladder leading to the quarterdeck of a magnificent cruiser named "Birmingham". The appearance of a party of apparently ship-wrecked "Pongos" looking as if they had been brought in by the tide, and having the audacity to put their dirty feet on the scrubbed, polished and hallowed deck caused the Officer of the Watch to give a realistic impression of a man seeing his mother-in law write off his brand new car. We were summarily removed; returned to our small craft, which had not had time to move off, with instructions to take us ashore before we contaminated the entire fleet.

So bad did we look that when we did get ashore we were treated indeed as ship-wrecked survivors. No explanations were asked for; visits to the clothing stores and paymaster at the naval base resulted in our being rendered respectable again, with money in our pockets, and railway warrants for our journey north. After a meal came our instructions to depart, and we did – but not north. Our luck had been so good to date that we trusted that it would stay with us for the next few days, and so, by common consent, we gave ourselves three days leave; departed for our various homes, and agreed to meet up at King's Cross Station in three days time to all return to Scotland together. Luck meant avoiding the Military Police, and it held.

I was therefore able to spend a few days in the luxury of my home in Cardiff, which I had not seen since the year before. I arrived in Fairwater completely out of the blue to the astonished looks of my parents, who had had no idea of my whereabouts. I certainly had a few stories to tell them!

7

TIME IN THE FAR EAST

Whilst Jim survived the Normandy Landings, thousands of others were not so fortunate, including Maurice Turnbull who went across on D Day +10. His platoon in the Welsh Guards were part of the massive invasion force whose job it was to make headway south from Arromanches into the Normandy countryside and to rid the area of any pockets of German resistance. All went well during July as Maurice and his platoon made steady headway towards Montchamp, a town which occupied a strategic location in Normandy and whose control was vital if the Allies were to press on south.

After waiting for back-up troops from other British and American brigades, Maurice and his men took part in an attack on the town in early August, and the Germans hastily retreated. But on the morning on August 4th, the Nazi's launched a counter-attack and a column of Panzer tanks advanced along one of the sunken lanes leading to the centre of the town. Realising that the tanks needed to be halted, Maurice and several others crawled alongside one of the hedges lining a lane running into Montchamp, hoping to throw grenades and other devices into the path of the tank. But just as the brave Glamorgan captain was poised to lob his grenade, the gun turret swung round and shot Maurice through the head, killing him instantly.

Maurice Turnbull

Despite his death, the convoy was halted and the counter-attack swiftly became another retreat, allowing other Welsh guardsmen to rescue the body of the Glamorgan captain and relay news of his brave actions back to brigade headquarters. The following morning, the dreadful news broke in South Wales about Maurice's death. By coincidence, a cricket match was taking place at the Arms Park involving many Cardiff and Glamorgan cricketers, and shortly after news of Maurice's death was posted on the pavilion noticeboard, the crowd rose to observe a minute's silence in memory of the man who had rescued Glamorgan from the prospect of oblivion.

The awful news duly reached Jim who, by now, was in North Yorkshire and being re-trained for the next phase in the War:

I was horrified at first to hear of Maurice's death and my mind swiftly turned to the grizzly scenes I had witnessed on the beaches in Normandy, before turning towards those calmer and far more peaceful days in the late 1930s when the batting of Mr. MJL Turnbull had held me, and countless hundreds enraptured at the Arms Park.

Maurice's death was a massive shock and a huge loss for Welsh sport in general. Like others I could have been forgiven for spending time wondering what Glamorgan would do without their inspirational leader, but after months of military training, it was the next phase of the War which occupied my thoughts rather than playing cricket.

Allied intelligence had indicated that the landings in Southern France would be virtually unopposed so we had been deemed unnecessary for that project and giving training for other tasks. Our job titles duly changed to Operators (Wireless and Keyboard), resulting in no more radio telephony or bashing the Morse key at thirty words per minute. Our jobs were much more sophisticated, punching out Morse symbols on paper tape, which was transmitted by automatic machines at ninety words per minute, and in turn receiving tape from the other end, and transposing it by means of a typewriter back into plain language or figure codes.

I had been posted again to the training school in Scarborough in North Yorkshire and after the horrors on the Normandy beaches, it was like living a whole new life. We were billeted in a requisitioned seaside hotel, and every day we had music. Literally so, because, as a means of teaching rhythmic form of typing, a musical beat was considered to be essential. Starting with a slow foxtrot, within a few months it built up to the rapid beat of the Post Horn Gallop, taking us up to the reasonable speed of forty words per minute. At least the Army taught us something that would be useful in civilian life.

Our new duties coincided with the formation of mobile transmitting and receiving units called "Golden Arrows". These were spacious vehicles, almost looking like miniature furniture vans, and the intention was to use them at Army field headquarters. Preliminary training again took place in Yorkshire – this time in the small village of Holmfirth, which subsequently won worldwide fame as the location for the filming of the television series "Last of the Summer Wine". On this occasion, the unit was small, with a total complement of no more than a dozen men, and as a consequence, life was less formal, with discipline almost non-existent.

We stayed there until early May 1945 when – to coincide with V.E (Victory in Europe) day celebrations – we were sent on embarkation leave prior to a posting

Jim, standing extreme right, with colleagues at Catterick Camp.

to Allied Land Forces South-East Asia (S.E.A.C) which was stepping up the war against the Japanese under the inspired leadership of Lord Louis Mountbatten. Once again, we embarked from Southampton, although our accommodation in 1945 was far superior than the craft we had occupied the previous year, as we sailed on the former luxury liner "Cape Town Castle" of the Union Castle Line. Even so, the conversion from cruise liner to troop ship had seen the rich carpeting and furnishings being removed to make way for hundreds of hammocks, bunk beds, washrooms and toilets, which, even then, were scarcely adequate for the seething mass of humanity being carried.

Fortunately, no convoy problems were encountered and we were soon rounding the southern tip of Spain, entering the Straits of Gibraltar, and seeing for the first time the wonderful hue of the Mediterranean Sea, the charm and clarity of which has never faded, and has attracted me to that part of the world ever since. Nevertheless, the two-day storm that immediately encompassed us quickly showed that the travel posters were not always right; that grey skies can turn the water grey as well, and proved to be most depressing.

However, the weather soon changed back to normality and, as we got ready to enter Port Said and the Suez Canal, the sight of the huge sun rising amidst the mirror like stillness of the sea was worth a fortune. The peace and calm were almost overpowering, but what a contrast when we did enter the harbour. In no time, hundreds of small boats, vastly overloaded with goods of all types, and manhandled by lean, brown disreputable men, pulled alongside to the accompaniment of noisy exhortations to buy the products, while numerous youngsters, no more than a few years old, invited the watching troops to throw coins into the water, in order that they could display their expertise in diving for the money, and recovering the coins with their sharp white teeth.

Once out of the Suez Canal, we headed across the Red Sea where the temperature was so high that the slightest movement caused profuse perspiration to form all over our bodies, and brought us hours of misery, lassitude and inertia. To think that people actually worked in such conditions. It was a great relief to reach the Indian Ocean, where the choppy seas and cooling breezes were a godsend. Our port of disembarkation turned out to be the Indian city of Bombay with its seething masses, its noise, its tremendous atmosphere of eastern magic; flies; dirt; disease and poverty.

Jim, in India, in 1945.

Apart from our own kit, we had with us a total of eighty tons of equipment, including complex aerial systems. This had to be guarded as if it were gold. It was dumped in a massive quayside warehouse, and we with it. Our beds were the rough concrete floor, where we would lay surrounded by the never ending hustle and bustle of a typical port, and colonies of cat-size rats. We were there for a week.

Travel and see the world indeed. We saw India alright, journeying by rail from Bombay down to the southernmost tip. The equipment was loaded at the rear, and we were in the next carriage, which really is misnomer, as it resembled a cattle truck, and probably was. No rats this time, however, only cockroaches of a size which put those of the destroyer "Fury" to shame. When stepped on they burst like squashed tomatoes with the noise of a cracking nut.

The ALFSEA football team in Singapore 1946, with Jim kneeling, second left.

Two-thirds of the way down through that massive country, there was a twenty-four hour stopover at Madras, for the simple reason that the Indian railway had two different gauges. It was necessary, therefore, to unload our eighty tons of equipment, take it to a siding, and re-load it onto another wagon capable of negotiating the narrower gauge line to our destination. Our stop proved to be well worthwhile as during the spare couple of hours before re-loading, I went to the local cinema, viewed a flickering obscure film of uncertain age about nothing in particular, with much chewing and spitting of Betel nut undertaken by the inhabitants alongside me.

Suddenly, the film was replaced by a slide in English – news had just been received that the Japanese had surrendered because two atomic bombs had been dropped on their cities. Surely the war was over for us – or was it? Conjecture was rife. How soon would we be going back home? In my case, it was to be another eighteen months.

Despite the decision of the Japanese, we still had our work to do, and the first part of that was to present ourselves with our cargo at A.L.F.S.E.A, HQ in the hills at Kandy in Ceylon. We arrived at last, and were quartered in an Army barracks amongst the forests a few miles from the town centre. The weather in this high region of the island was most pleasant, and very different from the steaming heat of Colombo, three hours away by train.

There followed a busy time, with one of our first duties being the setting up of our high-speed wireless station, and making contact with the War Office in London, so many thousands of miles from us. When established, we had the task of sending, for hours on end, personal messages which the newly liberated Allied prisoners of war in Malaysia were allowed. For once, we could use plain language in our communications, as all hostilities had ceased. It was rewarding work, as we could appreciate the joy and elation of parents and relatives on receiving the information that loved ones, who in many cases had not been heard of for year, were actually alive and in good heart.

The four months spent in Kandy slipped away rapidly, as they tend to do when one is fully occupied. Leave as such was unheard of, but one or two twenty-four hour passes were used to full advantage, more often than not, by taking the three-hour train journey to Colombo, soaking up the sea and sand, and also the local brew; viewing wistfully from a distance numerous sparsely clad females belonging to the Women's Naval Services (W.R.N.S.) or the nursing services. Wistfully, because they also belonged to the commissioned officer class, or appeared to, and did not deign to fraternise with such lesser mortals as ourselves.

Now that peace reigned in Malaysia, and some semblance of order had been achieved, it was decided that our high-speed wireless unit should be transferred to set up "shop" in Singapore, and accordingly, we picked up our bags and baggage; hopped aboard a ship, and arrived at the former naval base in December 1945. The Japanese had previously taken the island so swiftly that there was no evidence of war damage; the place was thriving , and as cosmopolitan as one could wish to see, with its mix of Malays, Indians, Chinese, British and Burmese, and, for the time being, a large group of Japanese prisoners of war.

Our billets were in the peace time barracks at Changhi, where, from our first floor balconies we overlooked the infamous Changhi Jail, in which so many of our troops had suffered for so long. Now roles were reversed, in that the many thousands of Japanese troops were put to work all over Singapore Island. At daybreak they were marched in long lines from their prison compounds to their places of work, and marched back again in the early evening. Most of them were employed in re-building the air strip at Changhi, and we were given the use of a couple of dozen of them for general duties around the barracks. It must be said that they were not afraid of hard work, and they were to be seen enthusiastically attacking even the smallest tasks presumably because they considered themselves lucky to be alive.

On one occasion we were taken away from the routine shift, and, as a small unit of four, set up a wireless out station alongside a beautiful tropical beach in the south of the island. Each day, our contingent of prisoners was marched in and were placed under our control. They looked after our every need and for us it was a real rest camp. Only a couple of hour's radio per day left us with plenty of free time to enjoy the sun, sand and sea. It was sometimes difficult not to fraternize with the Japanese – one in particular spoke reasonable English, and said that he had been a prominent musician with the Tokyo Philharmonic Orchestra. He was most obliging and, overhearing me express the wish that I had a small boat, promptly and efficiently constructed one, using a discarded aircraft fuel tank for the purpose. It floated; it was manoeuvrable,

Jim receives congratulations after the success of the ALFSEA team.

and the fact that I was nearly swept away by the strong current the first time I used it was not due to its construction but to my incompetence!

A partly wrecked brick building served as our sleeping quarters; it had originally been well-built, with its electric power and light cables set in conduit in strips of wood attached to the inside walls. One day, I noticed that one of these strips contained what looked like a loose piece of cable, but, as I reached in to remove it, there emerged from the end not the usual pieces of exposed wire but two rather nasty fangs. It was not loose cable, but a particularly venomous snake, which, fortunately, failed to make contact with me before being swiftly disposed of.

Our pleasant existence lasted three months or so. When it came to an end, and we returned to our main barracks at Changhi fit and tanned, we discovered that a full programme of sport had been organised. I was soon to re-discover my enthusiasm for soccer and cricket, the pursuit of which had been denied me, with the exception of a few odd games, during the past four years. Our signals unit formed teams to play against other forces units, and I quickly found that, in addition to the enthusiasm my ability seemed to be unimpaired.

There was no such thing as a separate soccer season and another one for cricket as both games were played as and when fixtures could be arranged, and it was not unusual to play one of each on the same day. One such occasion was widely reported in the local newspaper, and a copy found its way back to the "South Wales Echo". It reported the morning soccer fixture against another Army side – a handsome win for the Signals, seen by a keen band of supporters, and mentioning my contribution as the scorer of three goals, then, the afternoon cricket match, and the soccer pitch having been covered by a strip of coconut matting, which was the only true wicket available. A scratch R.A.F team were trounced, and my contribution was an unbeaten century. Not a bad day's work!

Eventually, the British Army team played a series of soccer matches at the main Singapore Stadium against teams comprised of Chinese, Malays and Indians. Each game was preceded by much advance publicity in the local "Straits Times", and tremendous interest was aroused. Needless to say, it was imperative that the Army gave a good account of itself for prestige and other purposes, but I played in every match and can confirm that the opposition, mainly the Chinese Eleven, proved to be very strong, and we were not always successful.

Throughout 1946, the process of repatriation and demobilisation was under way, and as each week passed, it saw the disappearance of friends and colleagues whose "demob" group number was lower that my 44 by virtue of their longer service. Gradually the magic figures went up and up, and then, in December, came my turn. At this time we had been moved from Changhi back to the city centre barracks of

Jim in 1945.

Tanglin, and after two or three days at a nearby transit camp we finally embarked on the liner "Georgic", a massive vessel of 27,000 tons, for the long journey back home to the back home to Britain.

We called at Bombay again on our journey home which, in all, took us a month. The thought of a month at sea in crowded conditions, with the interminable queuing for food and toilet facilities, was not pleasant, and I promptly volunteered for duties in the galley, ensuring that, at least, I should be working in comparatively uncrowded conditions. More than that, I would partake with the crew of the excellent fare that they enjoyed. So much for the compensations, but it was at the expense of spending many hours each day peeling mountainous piles of potatoes.

Eventually, the shop docked at Liverpool, and, before we disembarked, we beheld the sight of our gear being unloaded; the hundreds of kitbags being lined up on the dockside for our identification and collection. Mine was well stocked, not only with my personal belongings, but with a goodly supply of tinned food, and my war trophies, one of which was a magnificent Japanese officer's sword. Imagine my chagrin when, after checking and re-checking, and watching everyone else collecting theirs, I realise that mine was not among them. A search of the ship's hold proved unsuccessful, and I was led to the conclusion that the loading gang at Singapore had helped themselves before our departure. My sadness at the loss of this prize swiftly turned to joy on returning to home soil. But such was my inglorious return to Britain in January 1947, and in the middle of one of the coldest winters in history, I returned to Wales with nothing more than I was wearing.

8

PLAYING FOR GLAMORGAN

1946 had seen Glamorgan CCC take to the field again as county cricket resumed after six long and bloody years. There was some important re-building to be done, not least regards the captaincy following the death of Maurice Turnbull in Normandy in August 1944. Fortunately his great friend Johnnie Clay was still around and was both fit and willing enough to continue playing county cricket, no less than a quarter of a decade after his first County championship appearance during Glamorgan's inaugural year of first-class cricket back in 1921.

Johnnie was eager to build on the outstanding work of his late friend by helping to nurture a new generation of Glamorgan cricketers. Indeed, there were several new faces in the Welsh club's ranks as they resumed county fixtures, but there was still a nucleus of the team from 1939 with the likes of Emrys Davies, Willie Jones, Allan Watkins and wicket-keeper Haydn Davies all having completed their National Service and regularly available for the 1946 season. It began in mid-May with a defeat to Yorkshire at the Arms Park, but Johnnie Clay and his men bounced back with a thrilling three-wicket victory in the next game against Lancashire at Old Trafford.

After draws against Northamptonshire at Swansea and Sussex at Newport, Glamorgan recorded an emphatic innings victory inside two days over Sussex at Horsham, and all after being introduced at the start of the match to "Monty", or Field Marshall Bernard Montgomery of El Alamein who had commanded the Eighth Army in the Western Desert Campaign, and had been in charge of all Allied ground forces during Operation Overlord.

Glamorgan's players were delighted to meet the esteemed military leader, especially Wilf Wooller, their number three batsman on that day in early June on the South coast and a man who subsequently went on to great things as captain of Glamorgan. Wilf, together with Johnnie Clay and the other amateurs who were playing in this match, chatted at great length during the lunch interval on the opening day to "Monty", and Wilf would have dearly loved to have spoken more to the great tactician but for the fact that play resumed.

Wilf was the man who Johnnie Clay had identified as the next Glamorgan captain. Wilf had been born in North Wales and educated at Rydal School and Cambridge University where he won honours on the rugby and cricket fields before winning wider fame by being a member of the first Welsh rugby team to defeat England at Twickenham and then, in 1935, being a member of the Welsh rugby side that defeated the great All Blacks from New Zealand. Besides being a fine rugby player and footballer, Wilf was a more than useful cricketer and had played for

The Glamorgan squad of 1946 - Back Row: AJ Watkins, WE Jones, GL Davies, PF Judge, HG Davies, M Robinson. Front Row: AH Dyson, W Wooller, JC Clay, ADG Matthews and DE Davies

Denbighshire and briefly Lancashire's 2nd XI. In 1938, whilst working in the coal trade at Cardiff, he had made his debut for Glamorgan in Championship cricket, and the following year Wilf posted a fine century against the West Indian tourists.

Whilst playing for Glamorgan during his summer holidays Wilf had shown great promise with both bat and ball, although at this time, he regarded cricket only as a brief and jolly respite from his duties in the coal metropolis. Indeed, playing regular county cricket was at that time, far from his mind. But the War years however had dealt him a poor hand and he had been an Allied prisoner of war for almost three years in Changhi and other camps in the Far East. Fortunately, Wilf had been liberated by the time Jim visited the camp in the summer of 1945, The all-rounder however had lost much weight whilst in captivity and after returning to the U.K. in quite a delicate physical condition there was no way that Wilf would be able to resume his rugby-playing career. As a keen sportsman, he was looking for a fresh challenge and when Johnnie Clay spoke to him during 1946 about the possibility of taking over the captaincy of Glamorgan, Wilf jumped at the opportunity. It proved to be a very wise choice as he went on to mould a highly competitive and closely-knit squad who in 1948 – to the complete dismay of the London press – lifted the county title.

During 1946 and 1947, Wilf was also on the look-out for fresh new talent for Glamorgan and was eager to identify other home-grown youngsters to build on the work of Maurice Turnbull with whom he had played in the winter of 1932/33. Jim Pleass was one of the new faces in Glamorgan's ranks in 1947 – his call-up to county cricket however came as a bit of a surprise for Jim after he had started to adjust to life back in South Wales having returned from the Far East. In fact, if the truth be known, he would rather have heard from Cardiff City FC about an opportunity to play professional football.

How strange it was to be back in Britain, and to see the place-names, the signposts and the lighted streets and houses again. My train journey after embarkation at Southampton terminated at Wokingham, where we were directed straight to a demobilisation centre. There was, though, no waiting about here, as an assortment of civilian suits and clothing, plus footwear, was quickly distributed; railway warrants and clearance papers were soon provided, and I was on my way back home at last to Cardiff, almost five years to the day since that first train journey to Catterick. I had seen much of the world at His Majesty's expense; my outlook had broadened dramatically, but I wondered how much those five years had affected my all-time ambition to excel at sport.

After getting back to Cardiff, I made contact with my employers and swiftly resumed my laboratory testing work as if nothing had happened in the intervening years, linking up with old friends and acquaintances again. Much starved of female companionship for some time, I entered the world of dance halls, learnt to cope with the apparently intricate steps of the day, and generally tripped the light fantastic, enjoying both the gaiety and the freedom.

Now that life was back to normal once again, I was keen to consider a career as a professional sportsman. My footballing experiences during the War had proved that I had the abilities and skills to stand alongside the professionals, and having been on the books of Cardiff City and having kept in touch with the then manager Cyril Spiers during my period of military service by means of the occasional letter, I made my way to Ninian Park early in 1947 to see what might lay in store for me. Sadly, the result was not encouraging. A new manager was now in charge; the playing staff was larger than ever before, and, although I was invited to train regularly with them, there was no move to include me in any of the three teams.

Disenchanted and disappointed at the thought of not getting an opportunity to play League football, I swiftly turned to back to the Cardiff Corries and settled for the lesser skills of the local leagues, but the greater enthusiasm which prevailed on inferior pitches – where one changed in primitive accommodation and took cold showers afterwards simply because they were the only one available, could not dampen my disappointment.

Realising that my dream of being a professional footballer was not going to happen, I focussed my efforts on cricket and when the summer came around, I concentrated on securing a place in the Cardiff side. Having played before the War, I got an early chance to re-establish myself in the 1st XI, and had the good fortune to string together some useful innings. Cardiff CC always had – and still have – a good team, and a strong fixture list. Back in 1947 we faced decent opposition from South Wales as well as other leading teams from Gloucestershire and the West Country.

In common with the other county cricket clubs, Glamorgan were picking up the threads after the long break with a staff of seven or eight professionals providing the nucleus of the side, which was augmented by the inclusion of a host of amateur players who had caught the eye in local matches. To be brutally honest, it was a bit of a hit or miss arrangement, and resulted in many changes for the final XI. If one player failed, another was tried, but looking back I have to be eternally grateful as in June 1947, a telephone call came to my place of work from Johnnie Clay. During the course of the month, I had scored four hundreds for the Cardiff club against various teams from Gloucestershire and South Wales, and as a result of my success with the bat, I had been recommended to Johnnie as a promising batsman. His phone call however, was asking me specifically whether or not I would be able to travel by train on the Friday night to Derby to play for Glamorgan in the match against Derbyshire starting on Saturday, June 28th.

It was a joke surely? Someone was having me on. Although I had done well in club cricket, there was such a tremendous gap between that and county cricket, and surely that it wasn't possible for someone to be pitch-forked, without even a game for the 2nd XI, straight into the 1st XI and County Championship cricket. Johnnie assured me that it was no joke, and on Friday night I was on my way up to Derby. Many thoughts whirled around in my head during that train journey to the East Midlands. I had seen some of the famous Derbyshire professionals at the Arms Park before the War, and, indeed, I had waited seemingly for hours to obtain their signatures on, firstly, a scrap of paper, then, in later years, on a scorecard, or autograph book. Now it seemed I was going to join them as a county cricketer, although my abiding thoughts as my train headed north was that I would probably be twelfth man.

After arriving at Derby railway station, I duly made my way to the team hotel to meet Johnnie Clay. After booking in, I made my way to the bar and was soon introduced to Arnold Dyson, the Yorkshire-born opening batsman, as well as my boyhood hero Emrys Davies, who opened the batting with Dyson. Allan Watkins, Willie Jones and Wilf Wooller also introduced themselves to me as I stood, rather dumbstruck and surrounded by my heroes. But this was nothing compared to when Johnnie Clay then said "Welcome, Jim; you are playing tomorrow".

Everything thereafter seemed like a dream and next day, events moved so swiftly that there was no time to think or to wonder at the enormity of it all. Breakfast;

Jim in his Glamorgan sweater in 1947.

taxi to the Racecourse Ground, with its acres and acres of open space; changing into flannels; loosening up in the nets, and then the news that we had won the toss and were batting. Even more important for me after returning to the changing rooms was seeing that the prepared scorecards were showing the name of "J.E.Pleass" batting at number seven.

My delight though was swiftly tempered with realism as I quickly looked at the other side of the card and weighed up the opposition. Charlie Elliott, famous opening batsman; Dusty Rhodes, seamer and leg-spinner, whilst the nine, ten and eleven were George Pope, Cliff Gladwin, and Bill Copson, all of whom were England players and seam bowlers much to be feared.

The match duly started with Arnold Dyson and Emrys Davies opening the batting. By lunch three wickets were down, and I duly I sat with my pads on, listening to the dismissed batsmen and their comments; "It's moving about a bit – in the air and off the seam". Words probably used thousands of times by batsmen looking to excuse their errors, but hardly inspiring to one about to undergo his baptism in first-class cricket. At about three o'clock, and, with the fall of the fifth wicket, I found myself walking through the Members' Enclosure, past the pavilion gate, and out into the middle of the Derby ground and in front of five thousand spectators.

Before walking out Arnold Dyson had turned to me and said "Have a good look first, and then just play your normal game". Wilf Wooller was still in at the other end, and he greeted me with the same message as I found myself facing some of England's finest seam bowlers. It felt at first as if time had stood still; I found myself in the loneliest place on earth, out in the middle; massive men were hovering around my bat; no quarter was given, and there was no chance that I would be given one off the mark as an encouragement. No – this was county cricket and a real challenge. Although I was an amateur, I was representing my County, and I was determined to do my best.

It was a very steep learning curve but I had the good fortune to make 26 – the second highest individual score in the Glamorgan innings after Wilf's highly more combative 89. Understandably, I had begun quite tentatively but after finding that runs were perfectly possible to score I helped Wilf advance the total by at least fifty runs. It wasn't a bad beginning and although I was bowled by Gladwin, I returned to the pavilion believing that I had done my job.

Arnold Dyson kindly came over to congratulate me again after my dismissal, and when we batted again in the second innings, I again found runs relatively easy to come by as I posted an unbeaten 25 before the declaration came. I walked off feeling that I had not let the side down, even though a few hours later Derbyshire went on to complete a successful run chase and record a four wicket victory.

In all during 1947, I played seven innings for Glamorgan, and although my batting average was an undistinguished fifteen, I presumed that my continual selection meant that I had showed potential. With several veterans from the 1930s still playing, I discovered in later years that Johnnie Clay and Wilf Wooller had considered my swift fielding to be a major asset, and any runs which I managed to make were an added bonus!

At the end of the 1947 season, we undertook a tour of Pembrokeshire, during which we stayed in the ancient castle at Amroth. I was delighted to have been invited on the tour and on September the 4th, in a game against Pembroke, I made my first century in Glamorgan colours. Wilf Wooller and other senior players were very complimentary about my bating – something which greatly pleased me, especially as an amateur, I had specifically taken time off work to play in these so-called "missionary" games in West Wales.

With the cricket season now over, it was time to reflect and to take stock. Cardiff City apparently didn't want me, so if I was to pursue a career in professional sport, cricket was my best and probably only route. The opportunity had come my way in 1947 to play for Glamorgan, something I had always wanted; perhaps I should have done better; not been so impetuous at the wicket; waited for the loose ball; scored my runs more slowly, and spent longer at the crease. Had I blown it, or would there be another chance next year? The answer was not long in coming.

At the end of September 1947, I was laid low with influenza; aching in every limb, alternately hot and cold, and feeling very low when a visitor walked into my bedroom in our house in Fairwater. It was Glamorgan's Chief Coach, George Lavis – a fine man, who had been a source of encouragement to me and many other youngsters both before and after the War. He didn't waste time with preliminaries. "Glamorgan are prepared to offer you a summer contract as a professional next season, at a salary of £6 per week for 22 weeks. Are you interested?" Little did he know that the question was superfluous. I would have taken it for nothing. It was less than the money I was getting with the boffins at the tarmac company, and despite there being no guarantee that the cricket contract would be renewed or no guarantee that I would get into the 1st XI, how many people would have liked to have been in my shoes at that precise moment? Literally thousands. Naturally, I accepted with alacrity and my career as a professional sportsman began from the unlikely surroundings of my bedroom in The Drive, Fairwater.

Jim practices his forward defence stroke at the Arms Park.

9

COUNTY CHAMPIONS

Wilf Wooller was a bit like Marmite – you either loved him or loathed him. Those in the latter camp may have been put out by his outspoken and bellicose comments, but perhaps they misunderstood his intentions because everything which Wilf did was, at the end of the day, in the best interests of Glamorgan CCC. You could certainly not doubt his loyalty to the Welsh county after the Second World War given the countless hours of service he gave to the Club. Indeed, Wilf Wooller was the man who laid the post-war foundations and watched the Club flourish in 1948, when under his astute leadership, they won the County Championship title, to a mix of shock and dismay from the rest of the cricketing world.

After his decent start in Championship cricket during 1947, Wilf had high hopes of Jim, both as a batsman and as a cover fielder. Indeed, during his first summer in county cricket Jim's swift running and catching had helped to compensate for some of the more gentle efforts in the field by some of the more senior members of the team. Jim had also shown a very safe pair of hands when asked to field close to the wicket, so with Allan Watkins at leg-slip and Wilf at forward short-leg, Jim was frequently asked to slot in between them in the leg-trap as spinners Johnnie Clay and Len Muncer weaved their magic with the ball.

After recovering from the bout of influenza in the autumn of 1947, Jim was overjoyed that his dream of being a professional sportsman had finally come true. During the winter months of 1947/48 he kept himself fit with soccer every week for Cardiff Corries, and went to work each day with the asphalt company with great enthusiasm only because he knew he wouldn't have to do it for much longer.

My new life as a professional sportsman began in the first week of April 1948 with a letter from Wilf Wooller as the Secretary of Glamorgan CCC confirming my terms of employment. As a newly-signed professional player, I was to report for pre-season nets on the first Monday in April, at 10am, and this timely reminder soon had me searching in the darkest corners of my home in Fairwater for white shirts, flannels, socks, and the like. It soon occurred to me that I would no longer be able to rely on the communal use of pads, gloves and other ancillary equipment as in club cricket. As a professional, it was up to me to provide all my requirements, and to pay for the items. It transpired that I should probably need two or three bats, two pairs of batting gloves, four pairs of flannels, half a dozen shirts, vest, a dozen pairs of socks, and two pairs of boots; one pair with spikes for normal ground conditions, and one pair with crepe soles for use when fielding for several hours on rock-hard grounds.

Even in those days, the total cost of all this equipment was not inconsiderable. Problems did arise with bats – having spent some time in selecting the piece of willow, the weight and feel was all important, but there was no guarantee how long they would last. In fact, it was not uncommon for a bat to split up the middle within minutes of using it in the nets for the first time!

Reporting for duty on the first day of any new job can be a fascinating experience, and mine was no exception. The smell of newly-mown grass at the Arms Park; the distinctive odour of the nets themselves, newly creosoted; the freshness of the air; the sound of willow striking leather; the grunts of anguish and exertion as little-used muscles ached complainingly; the little knot of spectators gathered behind the nets at the Cardiff ground, watching every move with interest; the press reporters and photographers assessing and pictorially capturing the scene. These pre-season activities, consisting of batting, bowling and fielding for several hours a day for a period of three or four weeks from mid-April were ideal for getting into shape. Subsequently I found that, no matter how active I had been during the winter months; no matter how much exercise I had had playing football for Cardiff Corries, the first week of nets was always the worst, until ones' muscles had adjusted to the different type of activity.

Little did I know it, but 1948 was to be a key year in Glamorgan's history, and in my very first season as a professional cricketer I was to be a member of a historic side that in the opinion of some critics had the effrontery to take the County Championship title out of England. The season began on 5 May, with the opening game against Somerset at Newport, and it was soon obvious that the public, having been starved of good class cricket during the war years, had a willing appetite for Championship cricket. They duly turned up in their thousands, not only at our main grounds in Cardiff and Swansea, but also in the rugby strongholds of Neath and Pontypridd. It was not unusual to play in front of 15,000 at Swansea, and there is no doubt that this fervent support engendered an atmosphere which did much towards ensuring our success.

The pattern of summer life which unfolded in that year was to subsequently become familiar to me over the course of the next ten years. I had a basic wage, but those members of the team selected for the first match of a season had every reason to feel pleased, because it ensured extra cash, apart from consolidating ones' place in the side. The method of payment used by Glamorgan in the immediate post-war years was based around this basic wage, augmented by appearance money and win

The Glamorgan team and ground staff in 1948 during a friendly game against a local club. Jim is front row, third right, with Don Shepherd extreme left on the same row.

bonuses. At the end of the season, the Committee would also allocate a lump sum in direct proportion to the overall team performance, and this would be dispersed amongst the playing staff on merit. For example, an all-round performance of 1,500 runs and 80 wickets might have been worth an extra sum of around £40, while a struggling middle-order batsman accumulating 500 runs would have to be satisfied with a mere £5, as I soon found out from personal experience!

From the very first match of the summer, a cricketer's life is unique with a regular pattern of travel and play, as games alternate between home and away grounds. If he is married, it would not be too facetious for him to say to his wife: "see you in September," as the hours are long with players often returning late at night from an away game before having to be up early the following morning to travel to the next game at home. At this time, Glamorgan CCC still did not own their own ground, so besides the games at Cardiff and Swansea, they paid rent for the use of club grounds at a variety of locations across South Wales, including Newport, Neath, Pontypridd, Llanelli and Ebbw Vale. To reach many of these places a player based in Cardiff would have to leave home at the latest by seven thirty in the morning and would not return until after ten in the evening, especially as there were no motorways in those days.

The away matches meant long hours of travel by car, coach or train; more often than not it involved leaving one venue, with the match having lasted the maximum time, and reaching the next in the early hours of the morning; life was a continual round of packing and unpacking cricket bags and suitcases. On some occasions, when acting as twelfth man, I would be in charge of the baggage. My tasks included, in no particular order, organising the transportation of some twenty pieces of heavy luggage, tipping railway porters, cajoling taxi drivers to make mad dashes across cities from one station to another, with perhaps only seconds in hand before train departures.

One journey in 1948 still vividly remains in my mind. We were playing Yorkshire at Hull, and on the evening of the second day, with Glamorgan trailing by a substantial amount, it looked as though we should be able to catch an early train next day down to the Edgbaston ground in Birmingham, where our next game was. But, as usual, fate stepped in to dash our hopes – on the third day it rained until four o'clock; we passed the time playing cards, writing letters, signing autographs; the game re-commenced at 4.30pm; stumps were drawn at 5.30,pm and only then did we begin the interminable trip south. We arrived at Birmingham, snatched a few hours' sleep; reported to the ground at 10am, lost the toss, and spent a long weary day in the field. So much for the glamour of county cricket!

Reverting back to the duties of a baggage man, It was with a sense of achievement that, after travelling hundreds of miles, changing trains, bribing porters, purloining taxis from under the noses of other queuing passengers, one finally arrives at Trent Bridge, or The Oval, or Old Trafford, and safely deposits the lot in the dressing room. That is, until Wilf Wooller comes in, and, after looking around, says, "where's my cricket bag?"

Glamorgan's Championship-winning squad at Leicester in 1948. Standing: WE Jones, PB Clift, JE Pleass, AJ Watkins, WH Griffiths, BL Muncer, NG Hever, WGA Parkhouse and JT Eaglestone. Sitting: HG Davies, DE Davies, W Wooller, AH Dyson and G Lavis

Right from the early part of the 1948 season, Glamorgan were in the top three of the table, with the summer of 1948 starting with three victories in opening four games of the season as Somerset were defeated at Newport by 98 runs, Essex were beaten at Cardiff by five wickets, Worcestershire subsided to an innings defeat at New Road and Somerset crumbled to an innings defeat at Swansea.

Glamorgan then consolidated their position at the top of the table during June with a pair of remarkable innings by gifted batsman Willie Jones. The left-hander from Carmarthen struck two double hundreds in the space of a fortnight, starting with 207 against Kent at Gravesend, followed by an unbeaten 212 against Essex at Brentwood, and all during a record breaking partnership of 313 for the third wicket with Emrys Davies as the two West Walians confused their opponents by calling to each other in Welsh!

As the summer of 1948 unfolded, it became more and more apparent that we were doing rather well. On June 9th at Cardiff, my useful batting contribution of 77 not out against Hampshire helped us to a victory by 70 runs after the opponents were dismissed for 150 in their second innings. It was our sixth win of the season, and the mood in the camp was high as we travelled to Gravesend and duly completed an emphatic win against Kent, followed by another comprehensive victory over Essex at Brentwood. The stand-out feature of each victory was the batting of Willie Jones but he was so naïve and unsure of himself that, after these tremendous performances, he truly wondered if he would be picked for the next match. To see him in the dressing room before going out to bat; smoking numerous cigarettes held with trembling hand, one had the impression that he would never score a run, but, once in the middle, he was a man transformed.

By the beginning of August, Glamorgan had won eleven matches, and the race for the elusive title was intensifying, but our talented all-rounder Allan Watkins was then called up by the England selectors for the series with Australia. Our joy at the thought of Allan winning a Test cap had to be tempered by the knowledge that a most vital cog in an armoury was now missing.

In Allan's absence Wilf Wooller played the trump card by recalling Johnnie Clay to our side for the decisive game against Surrey at the Arms Park. Many to the east of Offa's Dyke thought that the loss of the all-rounder from Usk would signal the end of Glamorgan's title quest, whilst some thought the recall of a 50 year-old spinner smacked of desperation. But we proved these doubters wrong and Johnnie responded with match figures of 10/65 as we comprehensively defeated Surrey. He duly remained in the side for the next game at Bournemouth as we travelled to the South Coast knowing that one more victory would clinch our first-ever title.

Although the toss was won, only ten minutes play was possible on the first day because of rain and for a while a positive outcome looked extremely doubtful. After a break on the Sunday, and prayers from the Welsh contingent for sunny weather in the next few days, a full day's play was possible on the second day. Wilf duly encouraged the batsmen to quickly go for runs –"Bat and field like County Champions" was his message before play started and we responded in the best way possible, quickly amassing over 300 runs, and then taking six Hampshire wickets to put ourselves well on the way to victory.

The third day dawned bright and clear and to our delight Hampshire's first innings soon folded. They duly followed-on needing 231 to save an innings defeat, but by mid-afternoon, nine wickets were down for just over a hundred runs, and we were crowding round the last pair like vultures intent on their prey. Johnnie Clay was bowling, and, standing as umpire at his end was – of all people – Dai Davies, the former Glamorgan batsman who had retired after the War to take up umpiring. On that day at Dean Park, Dai was proudly wearing a red tie with a dragon motif, and when, in Hampshire's second innings, their last batsman Charlie Knott missed his intended stroke against Johnnie Clay, the ball cannoned onto his pads. The off-spinner immediately started a loud appeal but before he had finished the appeal, Dai had already said: "that's out and we've won".

Indeed, we had won; not only the match, but the Championship title as well, because Somerset duly did us proud by holding Yorkshire, who were breathing down our necks, to a draw with the net result that nobody could now catch us. We were county champions! The scenes at Bournemouth which subsequently unfolded were like a Wales/England rugby match; the singing of Welsh songs by the many hundreds of supporters who had made the long journey to see us; the speeches, the handshakes, and the champagne.

There were tears of delight running down the cheeks of several senior players as we gathered on the balcony of the Dean Park pavilion before getting together in the dressing room

The Championship-winning squad at City Hall, Cardiff in September 1948.

51

*at the Bournemouth ground to share a few words and to thank Wilf for his efforts.
He had been chosen to play in the match the next day between the Gentlemen of
England and the Australian tourists, so it was Johnnie Clay who led us back to
Cardiff General Station. It was nearly midnight when we eventually arrived, and
yet there must have been over ten thousand wildly excited Welshmen to greet us. An
impromptu party was then held at Cardiff Athletic Club, and it was with a weary
head that I scanned the newspapers the following morning just to confirm that we
had indeed clinched the County title. All in all, it was not a bad time in which to
start one's professional career as a cricketer!*

*HH Merritt greets Johnnie Clay and the victorious Glamorgan side on their arrival back
home at Cardiff railway station. Jim is standing second left.*

10

SPRINGBOK VICTORY

I t was with a great sense of Celtic pride that Wilf Wooller and his team travelled the country in 1949 as defending county champions. They knew full well that their victory in 1948 had met with more than a few scoffs from some of the traditionalists and several teams in 1949 seemed especially concerned to redress the balance and to make amends for the county title having left England.

But as Wilf was quite prepared to tell anyone eyeball to eyeball, Glamorgan's success in 1948 was not down to luck, and with some alert fielding and accurate bowling, especially on leg stump, the Welsh county had deservedly lifted the Championship title. There was also great joy in the Welsh camp in February 1949 when Allan Watkins, their popular all-rounder, became the first Glamorgan cricketer to score a Test Match century during the winter series with South Africa. The following year Gilbert Parkhouse, the talented batsmen from Swansea who had made his Championship debut in 1948 was called up by the England selectors. With Willie Jones and wicket-keeper Haydn Davies also appearing in Test Trials, it was proof that Glamorgan had come of age as a county.

After their success in 1948 Wilf's team finished in 8th place in 1949, and then 11th spot in 1950 before bouncing back up into 5th place in 1951 – a summer which also saw them record one of the most remarkable victories in their history as a first-class county, against the South African tourists at Swansea. In fact, Glamorgan were the only county side to defeat the South Africans on their 1951 tour, yet even the most partisan of Welshmen would have been hard pressed to forecast a Glamorgan win when Wilf Wooller's side were dismissed for a modest 111 after being put in on a rain-affected wicket.

The dramatic victory over the 1951 South Africans was, without question, the most exciting game that I ever played in. The tourists had brought over one of their strongest sides, containing many famous names – Dudley Nourse, Athol Rowan, Hugh Tayfield, Roy McLean, John Waite, Jack Cheetham, Clive van Ryneveld, George Fullerton; all these were international stars of proven ability and we knew we were in for a tough match in front of a massive crowd.

Jim cuts Percy Mansell in the match against the Springboks at Swansea in 1951.

Saturday, August 4th did not start too well for me. Huge traffic jams on the A48 to Swansea delayed me, and I arrived at the St Helen's ground just ten minutes before the scheduled start to find that Glamorgan had won the toss, and I was batting at number three. Really, I didn't have time to get my breath. Thirteen runs on the board, and our first wicket went down. The massive crowd did not bother me, but the swing bowlers did, and I soon edged a slip catch to Van Ryneveld, having scored just a single. After lunch, swing gave way to spin, and Athol Rowan, a world-class off-spinner, took us apart, the last wicket falling at the unluckiest of all cricket totals, 111.

It was some consolation, however, to observe that the ball was turning sharply, as we had high-class spinners in Len Muncer and Jim McConnon ready in the wings. In the space of the next ninety minutes, the crowd's disappointment turned to elation; South Africa, with their great batting line-up were 36 for 7. Then Athol Rowan, showing his own batsmen the right way to treat off-spinners, smashed a quick forty. Finally, Wilf Wooller bowled Percy Mansell, and they were all out – for the same total as us – 111. Tied on the first innings, and not a bad day's cricket for the spectators to savour. If only television had not been in its infancy, it could have been recorded for posterity.

With the St. Helen's wicket starting to take spin, Glamorgan's batsmen knew that they had to be positive in their approach. For his part, Wilf Wooller needed few invitations to attack the bowling, and if there was anyone who was not going to go down without a fight it was the Welsh county's leader. He hit a typically aggressive 46, and together with doughty support from Jim Pleass, Glamorgan were able to set the tourists a target of 147.

Sunday, thankfully, had been a rest day, and much given to thoughts about what lay in store for everybody when the match resumed next day. The Bank Holiday atmosphere at St Helen's was electric, Twenty-four thousand people had crammed into the ground; the weather was fine, and the wicket looked like a ploughed field. Glamorgan started their second innings, and as number three I was at the wicket within minutes, Phil Clift having departed with only three runs on the board. This time I had to get my head down and concentrate, which I did, and my 29 runs out of our total of 147 was one of my better efforts.

It meant the tourists needed just 148 runs to win, and nine hours in which to get them. Surely South Africa were the favourites and when they went to tea at 54 for no wicket, just 94 short of victory, many of the partisan Glamorgan supporters decided that they had had enough and made their way to the car parks to take an early ride home. They will never know what they missed. Within half an hour of the resumption after tea, South Africa were 54 for 1; 54 for 2; 61 for 3; 61 for 4; 68 for 5; 68 for 6 and 68 for 7 as Jim McConnon achieved a hat-trick.

The bottom half of the South African batting order had changed into "civvies", believing that they would

Wilf Wooller and Jim Pleass walking out to bat at Swansea against the South Africans in 1951.

not be needed, and, what with the mad scramble to change back into whites and don pads, their dressing room must have looked like the opening day of a quick-change artistes' convention. But the wickets kept tumbling – 72 for 8 and 72 for 9 before Percy Mansell was caught off a top edge, and it was all over. We had won the greatest match ever by 64 runs. Then the euphoria; we were mobbed: the Welsh National Anthem 'Hen Wlad fy Nhadau' was sung, and the champagne flowed. One consolation for those who had missed the game was that John Arlott, the famous radio commentator, was there, and his summary at the end was a veritable masterpiece, much appreciated by the listeners.

Some breathtaking catches had been taken close to the wicket, including one by Wilf Wooller at silly mid-on, after deflecting a firm on-drive from van Ryneveld and then clutching onto the rebound inches from the turf. Even Gilbert Parkhouse, fielding as substitute for Emrys Davies, took two fine catches, and all despite nursing a wrist injury. His second effort was holding onto a huge skier from Athol Rowan, and Parkhouse's catch ended this extraordinary match in Glamorgan's favour.

After the excitement of beating the Springboks at Swansea, it was back to the more humdrum games in the County Championship. Few of these contests got anywhere near matching the game with the South Africans as far as excitement was concerned, largely because teams were content to go on the field with one thought apparently uppermost; try and prevent the opposition from winning, even if it meant a tame draw brought about by an impossible declaration.

The great spoiler of cricket – rain – also seemed to fall in ever increasing quantities as the seasons rolled by, and the constant interruptions, resulting in long periods of time spent waiting about in dressing rooms, produced general apathy. All in all, these matters conspired to erode the enthusiasm. Wet wickets; wet flannels; wet boots; a few huddled spectators; it was a far different picture from those glorious days of 1948 in my early career as a professional cricketer.

There was another reason why I took great delight from the victory against the Springboks at Swansea, as it was a ground where I often struggled to pick up the ball when batting. Having a good sight of the ball is most important to a batsman, and today nearly every first-class ground has an adequate array of sightscreens. Not so in my day, particularly at Swansea. At the Mumbles End, where, incidentally, the light was better, there was a good screen, but at the Pavilion End, where the Members sat in tiered seats, it was felt that their viewing of the game was perhaps more important than providing the batsmen with a better sight of the ball. Consequently, there was a tiny sightscreen and one had to contend with trying to pick up the line and length of a delivery against a background of ever moving coloured hats, shirts and dresses.

Once, against India, I had accumulated seventy five runs, after which I, naturally, was seeing the ball well; their fast bowler Divecha then bowled a delivery that I never once picked up; it was lost against the myriad of colours in the background, and I only knew that it had been delivered when I looked behind me and saw the wreckage of my stumps. Another time, a similar set up. Prior Jones, the West Indian quickie, bowling from the same end, unleashed a snorter that knocked my cap off before I saw it, and the ball careered away to the boundary.

Despite the inadequacies of some of the sightscreens, I never felt daunted by facing these bowlers – in fact, I felt that too many County batsmen tended to be in awe of bowlers who had built up fearsome reputations. Whenever Glamorgan played against Northants and Leicestershire, invariably there would be dressing room discussion before the match. Would George Tribe be in the side? Would Jack Walsh be playing? These two were similar but unusual types of bowler, delivering a mixture of slow left arm leg-breaks and googlies which baffled the most experienced of batsmen. Emrys Davies could never "pick" them, and would often shape to cut a ball he thought was turning from leg stump to off, and suffered the embarrassment of seeing it move the other way. The leg-spinners like Jim Sims of Middlesex and Eric Hollies of Warwickshire also used to bamboozle us, probably because not having one in our side, we were so unused to playing them. Of the quick bowlers, Brian Statham, Frank Tyson and Fred Trueman were more than a handful, and were never mastered. The important point to remember, however, was that each one of these was capable of bowling a bad ball, which should be spotted quickly and dealt with by despatching it to the boundary.

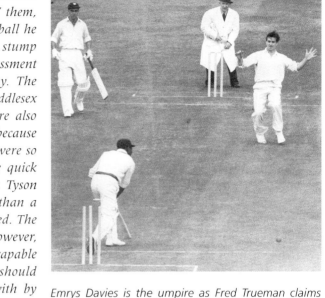

Emrys Davies is the umpire as Fred Trueman claims another wicket for England.

All batsmen have a favourite shot, and derive great satisfaction from executing it to perfection, whether it be a sweet cover drive, a delicate late cut, a sweep to leg, or a full blooded lofted drive. I was no exception, but with me it was the short ball, bowled on a slowish wicket, which sat up invitingly, and waited to be hit. I was ever ready to spot it; to get into position quickly, and to thrash it over the mid-wicket boundary for six. Two of the best leg-spinners I faced were Bruce Dooland, the Australian Test bowler, who played for Notts, and Doug Wright, Kent and England, but even they could bowl that loose one that sat up and waited, and it gave me immense pleasure to pull them both for six.

Once I varied the tactic. In the last over before lunch at Bristol, against Gloucestershire, John Mortimore, the off-spinner, bowled five good length balls, which I carefully played with a forward defensive stroke. Being rather fed up with the inactivity, I went down the wicket to the sixth, and hit it over the sightscreen behind the bowler. He was most upset; said that that sort of thing wasn't done to the last ball before lunch, and he threatened to report me to the Player's Union (in jest, I may add). When we met in future years, he would always playfully remind me of my show of bravado!

11

WOOLLER'S ARMY

Wilf Wooller was a ruthless and, at times, a very outspoken captain, leading from the front and never afraid to ask anyone to do anything that he would not think twice about doing himself. Indeed, Wilf was ready to anything in the side's best interest, whether it was opening the batting, bowling for hour after hour as a stock bowler, or fearlessly standing at short-leg, letting the opposition batsmen know what he thought of them!

Through a combination of application and tenacity, Wilf made himself into an excellent all-rounder and a measure of both his ability and durability was that in 1954 he achieved the coveted Double at the age of 41! A measure of the high regard in which Wilf was held, as a leader, tactician and a judge of a player, was that he acted as a Test selector from 1955 until 1962. No surprise, that during this time he helped to choose a highly successful England side.

Wilf Wooller stands at short-leg with Haydn Davies behind the stumps as a Leicestershire batsman drives through the off-side at Ynysangharad Park in Pontypridd in 1950.

But Glamorgan Cricket was his number one love – in fact, Wilf lived and breathed Glamorgan Cricket, fulfilling almost every role within the Club, from player to Secretary and latterly as President. Many of his critics rather misunderstood his intentions, not realising that everything Wilf did was, at the end of the day, in the best interests of Glamorgan CCC.

The Glamorgan side take to the field at Swansea in 1952. Wilf Wooller is fifth left with Jim second left.

Indeed, it was Wilf who, during the mid-1950s, argued fervently with officials of Cardiff Corporation about the need for Glamorgan to create its own base at Sophia Gardens instead of renting the Arms Park. At the time, the city fathers were considering other sporting avenues for the use of Sophia Gardens, including a new racecourse for the Welsh capital, but Wilf's plan for a centre of excellence for Welsh cricket failed to win their vote. That was until the early 1960s when it looked like international rugby might move away from the Arms Park to a site near Bridgend. Fearing the impact that the loss of international rugby might have on the local economy of Cardiff, the plan to develop Sophia Gardens resurfaced, and in subsequent months, the plan for the creation of National Stadium at the Arms Park resulted in the cricket section of Cardiff Athletic Club migrating a mile or so to the north at Sophia Gardens. It must have been with a bit of a smile on his face that Wilf duly oversaw the inaugural county game at their new Cardiff ground in May 1967.

Wilf Wooller was a colossus among men and captains, with the ability to lead by example; to drag up by their bootlaces a side of average talent so that each individual on occasion could play above himself; all of these things, but, at the same time, stubborn, domineering, and distinctly lacking in tact; a person whose word was law, and who did not take kindly to anyone contradicting his opinion.

Indeed, he and I had many a harsh word to say to each other, probably because I was never one afraid to voice and opinion, which, in retrospect, may have had a detrimental effect on my progress. He was not one to bear malice, however, but it is conceivable that he would prefer to have someone in his side who was more prepared to suffer his occasional outbursts without comment. Two other players who crossed swords with the "Skipper" were Stan Montgomery and Jim Pressdee, who, but for the clash of personalities, I feel sure would have stayed longer in the first-class game.

During his tenure as Club captain from 1947 until 1960, Wilf oversaw the emergence of a tough and competitive Glamorgan side, which was a far cry from the motley assortment of amateurs and professionals who played for the Club back in the 1920s and early 1930s. With Johnnie Clay at his side in his early years, Wilf continued the policy of giving local talent a go, but he also made some shrewd acquisitions from other counties, as he assembled a fine army of men, as Jim – one of his foot-soldiers – vividly remembers:

Johnnie Clay was an autocrat and true gentleman; he skippered the side in the 1940s when Wilf was unavailable, but he was far too nice to be a good Captain – quiet, almost diffident, but with a puckish sense of humour and ready wit evident to those able to see beneath that stern exterior. His vast knowledge of, and experience of, county cricket had been invaluable to Wilf and the pair had spent many long hours together in 1946 as Johnnie passed on a series of tips to the captain-in-waiting.

Remarkably, for a professional sport which was overshadowed in Wales by rugby and football and was rather an exclusive occupation, we had Phil Clift and Allan Watkins, who had lived a stone's throw away from each other in the small Gwent town of Usk. Both had been on the Glamorgan staff during the late 1930s; Phil was a hard-hitting opening bat with a lot of talent, who cared not for the reputations of bowlers. Indeed, on one occasion he made Ray Lindwall, the great Australian fast bowler, look very ordinary at St Helen's, and he earned high praise from the opposition. He was also a very fine close-to-the-wicket fielder, and, but for a serious illness would surely have gained greater recognition. He happily recovered, and, after his playing days, Phil gave magnificent service to Glamorgan CCC as chief coach, nurturing many Welsh youngsters up through the big gap between club and county cricket. He later became Club's Secretary, and performed the task with his usual supreme competence.

Allan Watkins was one of our finest all-rounders, being a solid middle order batsman always capable of leading a recovery if early wickets had fallen, by means of a sound defence as well as a batsman who could play quality attacking shots, and someone who possessed superb concentration. His immaculate medium-pace bowling, using swing and seam, was often a match winner, while some of the catches he took at leg-slip bordered on the incredible. He fully deserved his elevation to Test Match status where he proved to be a most capable and popular all-rounder.

The two Davieses, Emrys and Haydn, were senior members of the team, and they too both hailed from the same neck of the woods – that great rugby stronghold of Llanelli. They were not though related – something that swiftly became apparent as they were vastly different individuals. Emrys, a kindly, lovable, unobtrusive man, who gathered his fifteen hundred runs or so, and bowled his couple of hundred overs each season with a minimum of fuss; who never so much as raised his voice; who never complained about a doubtful dismissal; a professional to his fingertips, and a fine ambassador for his country, was an example to all.

Haydn was an articulate

Jim stands at second slip as Haydn Davies appeals for a catch.

graduate from Aberystwyth University who, because of his stocky build had the nickname of "Panda". He justifiably earned a reputation as second-to-none

Jim fielding in the covers at the Arms Park in 1953 as Yorkshire's Don Brennan nearly sweeps a ball into Haydn Davies' gloves.

as a wicket-keeper; whose raucous appeal one might think capable of waking the dead; executed the occasional leg-side stumping so smoothly and efficiently that they brought joy to the heart of the connoisseur, and whose batting consisted of one major stroke; a mighty swing in the direction of mid-wicket, which, because of his superb eye, brought him many runs, primarily in fours or sixes, a state of affairs not to the liking of the opposing bowlers. A keen student of the game, and a fine tactician, Haydn would have made a good captain.

Far worse wicket-keepers have played for England and Haydn was most unlucky to have been at the height of his game at the same time as Godfrey Evans of Kent. Godfrey was the man chosen by England – a dynamic and gifted wicket-keeper, he played against us in the early fifties at St Helen's, Swansea. Kept in the field all of one blazing hot day, Godfrey kept wicket brilliantly, conceding no byes, and, in his irrepressible way, never stopped talking while Glamorgan rattled up a score of over three hundred, only losing a few wickets in the process. At the close of play, after a quick change and bath, he was the life and soul of the get-together in the bar, entertaining all and sundry in song and repartee until closing time. Not content with that, he carried on the good work in his hotel until dawn; snatched a couple of hours sleep; batted at number three for Kent next day, after we had declared, and scored 97 glorious runs before lunch!

Humour was never far away when Haydn Davies was performing in the middle for Glamorgan, and yet he was so deeply involved in every game; his keenness to accumulate victims from among the opposing batsmen was such that he considered any catch within thirty yards of the stumps to be his exclusive property, and woe betide any close fielder who dared to get in his way. At Swansea one day, an opposing batsman tried to hook a bouncer, got a top edge, and skied the ball between wicket and wicket. Without hesitation, Haydn yelled "mine", came out from behind the stumps, charged up the wicket to get under the dropping ball, turned two circles while the ball spiralled down, missed it by at least three yards, and fell flat on his face. We also fell about – in stitches!

Another occasion involved Haydn and umpire Alex Skelding, a former Leicestershire fast bowler. Skelding was a tall man, who used to wear a trilby hat, glasses, white cricket boots, and sit on a shooting stick while at square-leg. He had a dry sense of humour, and was not content with a mere shake of the head when turning down and optimistic appeal. Alex's reply to a screamed "howzat" when the ball struck a pad or thigh would often be: "very painful, I'm sure".

On this particular day at Southampton, the Hampshire batsmen were building a big total in sweltering temperatures. The wicket was dead, and Len Muncer, who was bowling, thought he would introduce a spot of variety: just for a change he bowled a leg-break, instead of his usual off-break. The batsman went down the wicket to play it and missed the ball; Haydn whipped off the bails, and roared his appeal to Alex, who was sitting as usual on his shooting stick at square-leg. Nothing happened; it was as if the world suddenly stood still. There was no response, because Alec was fast asleep. By the time he jerked awake, the batsman was back in his ground, and was given "not out". Haydn's face was a study!

The London contingent, as they became known, were the imports from Middlesex: Len Muncer, Norman Hever and Jim Eaglestone. All three played a part in the winning of the Championship title in 1948, with Len and Norman each playing decisive roles, Jim though never quite made the grade. Len was affable, sartorially *elegant, but with an occasional chip on the shoulder attitude towards committee authority, believing that he was entitled to more consideration and much more money (and who is to say that he was wrong?). Norman was a lover of life; the bright lights and liquid refreshment, but whose in-swing bowling, even after a night on the tiles, frequently broke the opposition's early batting, and made the way much easier for the following spinners.*

Gilbert Parkhouse, the Swansea-born product of Wycliffe School, proved to be a quietly spoken introvert who chose his friends and companions carefully, and did not suffer fools gladly. We had similar views on many things, and it seemed quite natural for us to be linked together when playing away, and when the "who shares with whom?" questions were resolved when booking into hotels. The captain, senior professional and scorer would take the available single rooms, leaving the rest of us to sort ourselves out in the "doubles". Gilbert had that rare quality which earmarks a top-class batsman; an apparent ability to see the ball much quicker than anyone else, and, consequently, never being hurried into a stroke. His Test career was a success, and many of us thought that, had he been playing for a more "fashionable" county than "out-in-the-wilds" Glamorgan, his International appearances would have been far more numerous.

Willie Jones epitomised all that a cricketer should not be; at least in that period spent watching and waiting for a wicket to fall, knowing that he would be in next. He displayed an utter lack of confidence, and did nothing to uplift the morale of his fellow players who were closeted with him. He would literally shake with fear and trepidation, and yet would go out ultimately to display his superb gift of batsmanship, in which he would scorn the stereotyped methods of others by stepping back to the leg-side, and making room for his favourite shot; a sizzling square cut which sent the ball to the boundary. Given the self-confidence of a Compton, and believing in himself a little more, he would have been a world beater. He only really overcame his timidity after a few glasses of ale had removed his inhibitions temporarily; on such occasions he would stretch his 5 feet 4 inch frame, walk up to Wilf – the biggest man in the side – and say: "come on Wooller, let's go outside so I can show you the proper way to kick a rugger ball !"

Wilf was a great strategist and through his influence Glamorgan became one of the first teams after the war to realise the importance of everyone playing their part in the field. We each had our appointed positions. Willie Jones was our boundary expert – he would often run like a hare to cut off what looked like certain fours, as well as catch almost everything hit in the air towards him. Allan Watkins and Phil Clift were specialist close-to-the-wicket fielders; never flinching; never resorting to the present day uses of protective headgear, and often taking superb catches to boost the figures of Len Muncer and Jim McConnon.

My own preference was for cover-point; watching the angle of the bat as the stroke was played to assess where the ball was likely to come. Apart from saving

Glamorgan 1954. Standing: B Hedges, JE Pleass, BR Edrich, JE McConnon, DJ Shepherd, and WE Jones. Sitting: WGA Parkhouse, HG Davies, W Wooller, DE Davies and AJ Watkins.

boundaries, the fielder at cover was also expected to deny batsmen a single, and occasionally a real cat-and-mouse situation would develop. The batsman would play gently forward on the off-side, looking for a short single. Cover would have been fielding deep while the bowler was running up, but would come in very quickly at the last moment to give himself the chance of a run-out. From time to time, especially at the start of a batsman's innings, I would stay deep, allowing him to take an easy single. When he next played a similar shot, and moved off for another run, I would have come in on the burst to trap him. There were many fascinating encounters of this nature, which probably finished even, as, for all the times as I ran somebody out, there were equally as many when, throwing at the bowler's end, with only one stump to aim at, I tended to miss. It meant, though, despite many long hours spent in the field, that there was never a dull moment.

There is little doubt that Glamorgan's emphasis on fielding put us on the road to success and the Championship title in 1948. Each day, we would warm up before a match had started, practising catching, running and throwing, and what was significant, when one compares those days with the present, is that we were never still. Today, with the fall of a wicket, the fielding side tend as one man to sink onto the grass in an attitude of relaxation; for us, it meant rushing in to form a ring of fielders, throwing the ball from man to man, often employing sleight-of-hand; maintaining our reflexes, and revelling in the activity.

However, despite this show of dedication, and, despite the taking of many superb catches, there were always times when things went wrong; when catches were spilled, when run-outs were missed. Whenever I hear the words "catch it", I think back to some very excellent ones I was fortunate enough to take, and to a match, early in my career, at Derby, which proved the exception to the rule. We had removed most of the opposition reasonably quickly, and the immediate object was to dismiss the tail-enders before they could "cut and carve" their way to a respectable total. George Pope, the

Derbyshire and England fast bowler, did not believe in wasting his time when he was batting. Rather in the village-green-slogger mode, the high and mighty swipe was his stock in trade. Wilf Wooller decided to give him a few teasers to tempt him, and despatched me to the long-on boundary, right in front of the Member's pavilion, with my back against the rails.

Sure enough, George was tempted, and I saw the ball climb steeply into the blue heavens and almost suspend itself for a moment, before dropping with ever increasing speed

Wilf Wooller takes another catch against the Springboks at Swansea in 1951. Also shown are Allan Watkins, Phil Clift and Jim, with the bowler Jim McConnon, in front of the umpire.

right into my hands – and straight out again! It hit the ground between my legs, and went for four. Raucous laughter from the Members; a broad grin from George Pope; a smirk or two from my team mates, but not from the bowler, and the game re-commenced. It surely couldn't happen again; what is said about lightening not striking twice? It could, and it did. This time I had to move about ten yards to my left, but the ball went up so high that there was ample time to get under it. I lined it up; waited patiently again for it; it dropped to earth, and I never even laid a hand on it as it evaded my desperate attempts and went for another four.

The shame; the ignominy. To make it worse, when the laughter (which was louder), the broad grins (which were now guffaws); the smirks (which were now grins), and the glowering malevolence (from the bowler) had ended, some well-meaning character in the Members' enclosure threw his hat towards me, and said; "why don't you use that next time." As if there would be a next time, but there was! Two overs later, up went the ball into the blue, and it was quite obvious to me where it was going to drop. This time, though, it was a happy ending. I clutched it to my chest, and redeemed myself somewhat, but I never want to re-live the ten minutes that had gone before. Why had it happened? I was fit; I was confident; I was young (but felt much older afterwards); I was competent; but someone, somewhere, decreed that I should drop two easy catches at that time. Thankfully, it did not happen again!

12

A HUNDRED AT HARROGATE

In this modern era of central contracts, and players signing deals with county teams for two or three years, it seems hard to think that back in the late 1940s and 1950s Jim was quite happy to accept year after year just a annual contract with Glamorgan. Jim though was not alone in having this contractual arrangement as many other professionals also had rolling contracts. With Jim establishing himself as a regular member of the county's squad, and developing a good rapport with the rest of the squad and captain Wilf Wooller, the lack of any medium or long-term job security did not enter his head.

After the great success of 1948, his main thoughts turned to the award of his county cap – the tangible sign that you are a permanent member of the side and the reward for consistent efforts in the 1st XI. But for the next few years, despite being chosen in the 12-man squad, Jim was often in and out of the side

But in the early 1950s Jim secured a regular berth in the side and on July 28th, 1953 he was presented with his county cap after the match against Middlesex at the Arms Park following an unbeaten 75, batting at number six, on a wicket taking sharp spin as Glamorgan secured a first innings lead in the drawn game. He was now proudly able to wear the Club's cap and sweater with a daffodil in bloom rather than one in bud, as worn by the uncapped players. This subtle, and very clever distinction between the more experienced and irregular members of the side – comprising both amateurs and professionals – had been the brainchild of Maurice Turnbull who in 1933 changed the club's colours to blue and golden yellow, with a daffodil emblem replacing the red dragon motif.

Previously, the Club's colours had been green and red, with players wearing a green cap with a red dragon. These colours and emblems had been in place since the Club's Minor County days before the Great War when, with a limited fixture list and a vast number of amateurs making occasional appearances, the practice was to award a cap to a player after six games for the Club. This anachronism over the ways caps were awarded continued until after World War Two when, under Johnnie Clay's guidance, they were awarded on merit by the captain after a particular innings, bowling feat or a series of outstanding performances in the field.

It was a proud moment for Jim to be able to wear a cap with a daffodil in bloom, and even his salary rose slightly. But there were still other concerns on Jim's mind, especially the fact that he had yet to establish a regular place in the batting order, and especially had yet make a century for Glamorgan in the County Championship.

I was the one who Wilf Wooller left out of the side if it were decreed that an additional bowler was required, and, even when I was included, I may be batting anywhere from number one to number nine in the order. How different it might have been if I had been given half a dozen matches, batting at three, four or five.

As a batsman, I had scored by thirties, forties, fifties, sixties, and seventies, but when was that elusive maiden century coming – if at all? Losing my wicket when well-set was becoming far too common an occurrence, and in the main it was entirely due to either an injudicious stroke or a lapse in concentration. As some of my colleagues commented, it hardly ever resulted from receiving an unplayable ball.

The answer clearly lay with me and my mental approach, and I was determined to do something about it. My chance duly came on Saturday, 1st July, 1950 when Glamorgan were at Kettering, playing against a Northants side skippered by the great "John Bull" type – F.R. "Freddie" Brown. The ground was a small one, situated on the outskirts of the market town, and the boundaries looked invitingly near. Glamorgan won the toss and batted, but at 120-5, when I joined Gilbert Parkhouse, the future looked very insecure. However, careful application rectified the position, and the runs began to flow. A careless shot to deep mid-wicket was nearly my undoing, but the fielder misjudged it, and put the catch down. Gilbert was dismissed for 62, but I went on merrily past my fifty, and the maiden century was looming on the horizon.

Tea had come and gone, and I happened to look at both the scoreboard and the clock. It was twenty minutes to seven, with twenty minutes left for play, and my score was ninety six. Four runs to go, and all the time I needed. The most important thought, of course, was not to throw the chance away; to wait for the loose ball that would surely come along. Freddie Brown had different ideas; for that long twenty minutes he kept me at one end by means of several overs of perfect length balls; never deviating from the line of the stumps, and with a defensive field that could not be penetrated. Never mind, my colleagues told me at the end of the day; when the match resumed on the Monday morning it shouldn't take me long to achieve my goal. All day Sunday I kept wondering how those four runs would come. Perhaps a pull to leg or a square cut to the boundary?

On Monday morning came the anti-climax. It rained, and it rained, and it didn't stop. There was no hope of play, and the game was called off for the day just after lunch. Still, there was always Tuesday, and when it dawned with clear skies, and the drying out process began, it was apparent that we should have some play during the afternoon. Just before the lunch interval, the captains decided to make a start after inspecting the wicket; Wilf Wooller then put his head around the dressing room door, and said: "Sorry, Jim, but I've declared". Ah well, I thought, there'll always be another day.

It duly did, but not until 1955 during a remarkable match at Harrogate as Glamorgan recorded their first ever victory on Yorkshire soil. What made their win even more creditable was that Glamorgan were without their inspirational leader Wilf Wooller, and had arrived in Yorkshire on the back of consecutive defeats to Hampshire and Leicestershire.

In fact, Glamorgan only just avoided the follow-on in their first innings after the home side had batted well on the first day, with Billy Sutcliffe and Doug Padgett dominating proceedings with a stand of 138 for the third wicket. Jim Pressdee caught and bowled Padgett when the Yorkshire opener was in sight of a hundred, but Sutcliffe remained undefeated on 161, hitting three sixes and twenty two fours. It was not long before Glamorgan were in trouble, subsiding to 40-4 with Willie Jones being the only specialist batsman to offer any resistance against the accurate Yorkshire attack. When the experienced left-hander was finally dismissed by Brian Close for 79, Glamorgan were on 189, and still short of the follow-on.

Against almost everyone's expectations, Hugh Davies and Don Shepherd then shared a remarkable last wicket stand of 56, with Shepherd unleashing some furious blows to take Glamorgan past the follow-on target. His brave fusillade eventually ended when Norman Yardley recalled Philip Hodgson into the attack, and the opening bowler had Shepherd caught behind by Jimmy Binks for 48. Despite this tail-end resistance, Yorkshire still had a first innings lead of 136, and by the second evening, they had extended their lead past the 300 mark, thanks to some aggressive blows from Vic Wilson and, for the second time in the match, Doug Padgett. Eventually, Norman Yardley set Glamorgan a target of 334 on the final day, and with spinner Johnnie Wardle taking the first four wickets, a Yorkshire victory looked on the cards.

Jim Pressdee and I though had other thoughts. The wicket was good; the outfield fast and the Yorkshire team were becoming rather complacent. Evidence of this came early in my innings as one of their fielders dropped a straight-forward catch. Had this been us, and Wilf had been captain, the player in question would have received a withering look and some stern words from the Skipper. But to Yorkshire on that day, it all seemed a bit of a joke, but it was us who had the last laugh.

Jim and I got our heads down and made serene progress. All the wiles of Johnny Wardle, Brian Close and Ray Illingworth were of no avail, and after Jim had been dismissed Jim McConnon got stuck in as we slowly chiselled away at the target and made the bowlers tire. When, late in the afternoon,

The Glamorgan squad at Lord's in 1952. Standing: JE Pleass, B Hedges, PB Clift, BL Muncer, JE McConnon, DJ Shepherd and WGA Parkhouse. Sitting: AJ Watkins, DE Davies, W Wooller, HG Davies and WE Jones.

I leg-glanced to the boundary to record my first "ton", my cup was full. Shortly afterwards it was over-flowing as the winning run was scored, still with twenty minutes remaining. We had beaten Yorkshire on their home ground for the very first time, and they did not like it. They quietly and quickly packed their bags and left the ground with not so much as a "well played" – with one exception. Norman Yardley, the Yorkshire captain and ever a gentleman, had the courtesy to come into our dressing room and congratulate us on our achievement, but as for the others; all I can say is that they don't like losing in Yorkshire!

It was with a tremendous sense of exhilaration that I returned to Cardiff that Friday evening and, as is only human, I took a great delight in devouring the sports pages of the national and local daily papers the next morning, but there is nothing like this game of cricket to bring one down to earth.

In the afternoon, Glamorgan were committed to a friendly fixture at Merthyr Tydfil, against the Hoover Sports Club, on the occasion of the opening of their new ground at Pentrebach. To commemorate this event, a full strength Glamorgan side was selected. At 2pm I opened the Glamorgan innings, having been accorded a fine welcome after the many kind remarks made by the public address announcer, but at 2.02pm I was returning to the pavilion, having been caught for nought from the third ball of the match. "C'est La Vie", as the French say.

13

RETIREMENT FROM COUNTY CRICKET

I t is the hardest decision a professional cricketer, or indeed any sportsman or woman, has to make – when to call it time, and to retire. There have been many cricketers in Glamorgan's history who have bowed out on a high. One of the most notable was Hugh Morris whose final match for the Club coincided with the Championship-winning encounter at Taunton in 1997, where in what proved to be his penultimate innings for the Club, the doughty left-handed opener scored a fine hundred which helped to lay the platform for a wonderful and emotional Glamorgan victory against Somerset. Steve Watkin, the stalwart seam bowler also ended his career in 2001 when Glamorgan secured promotion into Division One of the National League.

In contrast, others like tearaway pace-bowler Jeff Jones in the late 1960s and gifted opening batsman Steve James in the early 2000s have been forced into premature retirement as a result of injury. There have been some – fortunately at Glamorgan a relatively small number – who have drifted on, desperate to continue playing county cricket and believing that their loss of form has only been a temporary blip, before the decision has been taken out of their hands by the Club's officialdom deciding not to re-engage them for the following season, leaving the person feeling bitter at what might be perceived as an injustice or personal sleight, claiming that others had been giving preferential treatment.

Fortunately Jim was not in this latter category and he did not leave the Club feeling bitter or resentful towards others. Instead, Jim took the decision himself in 1956 to call time on his county career with Glamorgan

To be perfectly frank, I had become completely disenchanted with my in and out form as well as the fact that I did not have a regular spot in the batting order. Considering that by this time I now had a young wife and family needing my support and presence, I made the decision to retire from the professional ranks. The Glamorgan committee accepted the situation, and I was free to make a new life in the world of commerce, which at least offered me the prospect of a secure future.

Professional cricket was, and to a large extent still is, something of a lottery; players are only as good as their fitness and form allows, and, in the event of the lack of either, there is always someone ready and willing to take to place open to them. Until recent years, indeed, some say, until the advent of Kerry Packer, county cricketers were quite poorly paid, but, in fairness to the county administrators, there has never been that much in the kitty anyway.

Limited-overs cricket, and the appearance of generous sponsors has, at least, made the occupation less precarious, whereas, in our

The Glamorgan squad at Trent Bridge in 1956. Standing: JE Pleass, KH Lewis, JS Pressdee, PM Walker, LN Devereux, B Hedges and DJ Ward. Sitting: WGA Parkhouse, HG Davies, W Wooller, AJ Watkins and DJ Shepherd.

day, the golden egg was denied to many. It came in the form of a Benefit Match or season, but only then to those who had managed to survive the pressures and competition as a capped professional player for at least ten years. However, the large amounts of money that are collected for beneficiaries today do represent a more than useful tax-free nest egg.

What a change from my early days, when players who had given marvellous service to Glamorgan, and in some cases had helped them to win the Championship, were given a Benefit Match during the season, but not all the proceeds were theirs – they first had to pay the general expenses of the game, which comprised catering, gatemen, publicity, advertising and the like. Very often the remaining balance would be less than two thousand pounds, if the weather happened to affect the game; the Beneficiary had to pay the cost of what was called pluvius insurance. It is true that one famous Glamorgan player, when offered a Benefit Match by the Club's committee, turned it down, saying that he didn't think he could afford it!

It is, perhaps, not surprising that I, having been capped for three years, but still in and out of the side, could see no future in the game, especially when there were talented youngsters like Alan Jones and others waiting in the wings. When I left, at least I was the possessor of a host of happy memories. What had I achieved in county cricket? I had made many useful scores; contributed greatly in the field as a specialist cover point; ended up with over four thousand runs and some eighty catches; had been a member of a Championship-winning side; I had been eulogised, feted, castigated, booed, cheered, wined and dined with Lord Mayors and other civic dignitaries; met *many titled and influential people; and received a letter of congratulation from the Inland Revenue Cardiff staff on the occasion of my century against Yorkshire!*

I had played on all the major grounds in England and Wales – Lord's, The Oval, Old Trafford, Trent Bridge, Edgbaston. I had played against such renowned cricketers as Len Hutton, Cyril Washbrook, Jim Laker, Trevor Bailey, Denis Compton, Bill Edrich, Tom Graveney, Harold Gimblett, Arthur Wellard, and hundreds more, and also against all the great touring sides –Australia, New Zealand, South Africa, West Indies, India and Pakistan; sides containing such names as Neil Harvey, Richie Benaud, Ray Lindwall, Keith Miller, Dudley Nourse, Athol Rowan, Sonny Ramadhin, Alf Valentine and the three W's – Frank Worrell, Everton Weekes and Clyde Walcott. I had lived with; shared dressing rooms and hotels with; played with; argued with; and laughed with my Glamorgan colleagues who had reached the heights of their profession, and those who had plumbed the depths.

Of the thousands of cricket watchers who watched my efforts for Glamorgan, many must have wondered what it must be like to actually take part in a first-class match; to wonder at the goings-on in a typical dressing room; how a player feels while waiting to bat; what it is like when he arrives at the middle. It is evident to me that, had some of these people been given the chance of experiencing these things, they would be wide-eyed with astonishment.

No matter how small, or how large, dressing rooms are the same the world over. Equipment scattered indiscriminately on chairs, on tables, on the floor. The over powering smell of bat oil; oily products to lubricate the body; masses of bandages, plaster, personal clothing, newspapers and magazines; a pall of cigarette smoke; players recumbent on massage tables, benches and chairs; putting on pads and gloves; in card schools; writing letters, or signing autographs; watching the game in progress and passing interminable comment on batting, bowling, field placing; the weather, the state of the wicket, and the umpiring, and, for those with binoculars, a prolonged study of the crowd, especially looking out for a few attractive, and hopefully unattached, girls.

The doors would be constantly opening and closing to admit disgruntled dismissed batsmen; ingoing batsmen, officials, committee members, and, occasionally, friends. Definitely not places to be recommended for those requiring peace of mind and a quiet period of preparation before going out to play the innings of a life time. It was my endeavour, on such occasions, to remove myself from that company and all those activities as often as possible, because, apart from the foregoing, a dressing room could be so dark as to require the help of electric light even in the middle of the day.

Far better, I thought, to sit outside in the natural light, and become used to it, rather than to try and adjust to it during the short walk from the pavilion to the wicket. That short walk was an important one; deep breaths, and not too hurried steps, did wonders to restore ragged nerves; and ragged nerves there were. No second chances out in the middle; the opposition wanted to see the back of me, and preferably first ball. All those people trying to intimidate me and get me out. Thirteen of them, including the umpires, as my enemies, and only one friend, batting at the other end.

Quite enough, one might think, to disturb the most equable of persons, but there would be more to come. A brief "morning" or "afternoon" to the nearest fielder; to the wicket-keeper, and the umpire; a request for guard: "two legs, please". Mark it suitably with a boot spike; a look around the field and a check of the fielding positions, then settle down

Jim, extreme right, nearly runs out a Nottinghamshire batsman at the Arms Park in 1956.

and wait for the first ball. Play the first couple back carefully and defensively, and listen to the wicket-keeper talking to first slip: "this chap looks a bit out of touch, the way he's playing. I don't reckon he's going to give us much trouble". And, very often, he would be right.

What would we have given to be a Denis Compton. Completely immune to the dressing room hustle and bustle, he would sleep peacefully in a corner; would more often than not have to be woken up and told that it was his turn to bat, at which he would be up as fresh as a daisy, say: "lend me your bat, old boy", and, "Can anyone let me have a pair of gloves"; stride purposefully to the wicket; take guard, and hit the first ball through the covers for four.

The problem when batting at, say, number six in the order, is that you never precisely know when you will be wanted, If Glamorgan lost two wickets fairly cheaply in the first morning's play, then I would put the pads on. A stand would then develop; Lunch would arrive, and off would come the pads. Back on after lunch, and I may or may not be required before tea. This happened once at Swansea; I had first put the pads on just before lunch. The intervals came and went; off and on went the pads. At five minutes to seven, I was still waiting. Since its early morning life, the wicket was playing perfectly, and we were amassing a very useful score, more than three hundred already. Then it happened; our fourth wicket went down, and I was in. Now, it is bad enough negotiating those never-ending steps at Swansea, walking down from the pavilion to the field, but when you have to do it twice within the space of a couple of minutes, and with nothing to show for it, it does nothing for one's *confidence. The very first ball I received, for some unaccountable reason, reared up off a length, flicked my batting glove, and landed safely in the hands of the wicket-keeper. The solitary consolation was that I had company on the way back. The fall of my wicket heralded the end of the day's play, and I was accompanied off the field and back up the pavilion steps by the opposing side, the umpire, and the not out batsman. Not that I felt any better for it!*

In my first-class career, which spanned ten seasons, I calculated that I walked out to bat no fewer than two hundred and fifty times, and yet the mixed emotions I experienced during my early innings were not dispelled by time. In fact, towards the end, I found that I had a marked reluctance to face the challenge that every fresh innings brought. It may have been because, over the years, I had not achieved the standard I thought possible. Each innings was a challenge, and a batsman, as now, needed a combination of skill, even temperament and good fortune. It really was remarkable how, at times, an innings developed from an inauspicious beginning.

Going in to bat, with the weather at its worst; grey, overcast skies, a cold wind, damp conditions; a jaded feeling, with maybe a slight headache; with the ball deviating in the air or off the wicket, and, even when contact was made, finding the edge of the bat, and lobbing gently far too close to the eagerly waiting slip fielders. Then it became an imperative to keep going; to forget the conditions and to concentrate utterly. I can remember such a time at Cardiff, when we were playing Middlesex. I played and missed; played and edged, and Laurie Gray, the so-aptly named opening bowler,

The Glamorgan team which played Nottinghamshire at Llanelli in 1955. Standing: BR Edrich, JS Pressdee, KH Lewis, DJ Shepherd, and JE Pleass. Seated: B Hedges, WGA Parkhouse, HG Davies, AJ Watkins, JE McConnon and WE Jones.

very nearly blew a fuse at the ill luck he was suffering. In one exasperating moment, when I was so nearly caught, he shouted down the wicket: "when are you going to hit the …….. ball with the middle of your …….. bat?" Next over I was down at his end, and in a position to reply; "Laurie, look at the score board (I was thirty not out). If I can get as many as that off the edge who needs the middle of the bat?"

Conversely, there was the time at Chichester, playing against Sussex on a beautiful summer morning. We had won the previous match; had won the toss; all was peaceful and serene, and I felt marvellous. The first couple of shots were exquisitely timed, and only superb diving stops at cover prevented fours. The next ball flicked the inside of the bat, clipped my pad, rolled back, and gently came to rest against the off stump, with sufficient force to dislodge the bail.

These were the days when Glamorgan played in excess of thirty three-day matches in a season but, as there were no limited-overs contests, Sunday very often was a day of rest. Very pleasant it was, too, to be able to have a lie-in; a late breakfast, and a generally lazy time, which did wonders for the ever under pressure professional, mentally and physically worn as he was after six weekdays of playing and travelling. There were occasional Sunday activities, either on a golf course or helping a colleague with one of his Benefit Matches against a club side, but these latter games were just gentle exercise, much like Jack Nicklaus playing nine holes against a twenty-four handicapper, and giving him no shots.

At the end of each season, Glamorgan would also organise a few matches on a friendly basis either in North or West Wales, and these "missionary" games tended to be on the same lines with more emphasis on the social side. One such match was arranged against a Royal Navy Eleven at H.M.S. Harrier, a shore station in Pembrokeshire. On arrival at the ground it became obvious that there would be no cricket. It had rained for days, and looked certain to rain for a few more. Instead of cricket, we were forced to accept the hospitality of the wardroom and, although I was not a drinking man, it seemed churlish to refuse the offer of the local tipple called A Horse's Neck. It was a combination of brandy and ginger ale, but for some reason it had no effect on me, and many hours later, I was handed a very attractive green and gold tie to commemorate the feat. I learned later that only three were ever given at any one time; to the last three persons remaining on their feet.

When these end-of-season tours were over, we returned back to our base in Cardiff; said "cheerio" to our fellow players; packed away our kit for the winter and made our way home to prepare for the long break. Some would truly hibernate, and not surface until the next April. Others would take advantage of the opportunities available to travel abroad; mostly to South Africa, where British professionals were much in demand to coach in the schools and to play in local cricket there. However, as a family man this never appealed to me as, having been apart from my wife and family for five months in the summer, it would have been grossly unfair to them if I disappeared for the winter as well.

Coaching did appeal to me, however, and I was able to do quite a lot at home. Glamorgan were still using the indoor school inside the North Stand at Cardiff Arms Park, and many a winter evening was spent in trying to raise the standard of schoolboys and club cricketers in that cold and draughty environment. My soccer career also flourished for a few years, and I enjoyed several seasons playing for Lovell's Athletic of Newport in the Southern League.

I also had a spell back in club cricket with Cardiff CC who I captained in 1958 and 1959. At first, I enjoyed the opportunity to keep my hand in playing cricket besides acting as captain and leading the side which contained several players who I had coached during the winter months in the nets which were hung along one of corridors of the North Stand at the Arms Park rugby ground. It was quite gratifying for a while to see these players progress, develop, and grow in confidence, but to be honest I increasingly missed the cut and thrust of professional cricket.

It had been a great honour to lead the Cardiff club and to help in the development of their young players, I stood down at the end of the 1959 season, besides cutting back on the number of games in which I would participate. I had been proud to skipper of a very good side which enjoyed great success, but disenchantment had increasingly set in because I realised that I was not getting much personal pleasure from club cricket. If I batted, and scored fifty, someone would say: "so he should; he used to be a professional with Glamorgan". If I failed with the bat, someone else would say: "what's wrong with him, an ex-professional too". That was it. I was thirty five years old, and I decided to make a complete break from playing and watching. It was time for my life to move in another direction.

Jim, sitting second left, with the Cardiff CC squad in the late 1950s.

14

A BUSINESS LIFE

I n the past few years, the England and Wales Cricket Board, in association with the Professional Cricketers Association, has created lifestyle advisors who help young cricketers adjust to the many and varied demands of life as a professional sportsman. For the older players, these lifestyle advisors and mentors also provide help with training and other courses which will give the players, some of whom have left school or college with minimal qualifications, the guidance they need in order to secure employment when their playing careers come to an end.

Jim, though, was from a different era and when his professional playing career ended in 1956, it was up to him to find alternative employment. Fortunately, he had a decent network of contacts and having worked in "normal" life before his call-up to Glamorgan in 1947, he was able to make contact again with his former employers in Ferry Road to see whether there were any opportunities of re-joining the asphalt company. Jim though was looking for

a fresh challenge, and, to his surprise, it came via his work during the winter months for the insurance brokerage run by Club captain Wilf Wooller.

It had never been easy to obtain employment just for the winter months. Admittedly, employers welcomed the opportunity of having someone on their staff who was in the public eye as a sporting personality, especially if the selling of a product

Jim in his office in the late 1950s.

were involved, but they were not so keen when it meant the granting of five months' leave each summer.

Initially, I was able to secure work as a temporary civil servant, but working daily in a centrally heated office block had its drawbacks, and there were occasions when I felt like a tropical plant in a greenhouse. The stifling heat and lack of fresh air could be unbearable, and my attempt to open windows met with strong opposition from the permanent residents, who had become, presumably, acclimatised to the enclosed atmosphere.

Eventually, I conceded defeat, and left for pastures new, which by a quirk of fate led me into something I vowed would never appeal to me – insurance. I had never given thought to following my father into this line of business but it so happened that Wilf Wooller was involved in an insurance broking firm that was looking for a representative, and he decided that I might fit the bill. For that I shall be happy to confirm my gratitude, because it opened up the way for my future career after I left Glamorgan.

In particular, working for Wilf gave me a grounding into an important service industry, and after I retired from playing for Glamorgan, I was able to secure a position with another and much larger insurance group. Admittedly, I had an offer to stay with the local broking firm on a permanent basis, but felt that my opportunities were limited with the company. My new employers, quite rightly, insisted that I should learn the business and for the next few months I was sent to their London head office, where I was given the technical knowledge without which the progress of an outside representative would be hindered.

Spending a week at a time in each specialist department was of great value, and I was able ultimately to return to Cardiff to take up my post of inspector with complete confidence. The five years I worked with the Northern Assurance Group were enjoyable; I had security; I had a guaranteed retirement pension; special house purchase facilities at a much reduced interest rate, and a group of very pleasant people with whom to share not only the working hours but also the numerous social activities. Of course, when the summers came along, there were times when I would look wistfully out of the window, and wonder how Glamorgan were faring against Lancashire at Old Trafford, or Middlesex at Lord's.

By this time, playing cricket and soccer had been discarded, but once a sportsman always a sportsman, and I had to find a new activity, preferably one where age was relatively unimportant, and which could be played all the year round and in all weathers. So it was that I was introduced to the game of golf. In the past, I had walked around various courses on Sundays with my cricketing colleagues, who were reasonable players, but I had never felt the urge to compete myself. All this changed when I was accepted for membership at the Llanishen Golf Club in north Cardiff.

Although I had read numerous books on the sport, I quickly decided that the style I would adopt would be my own, worked out by trial and error. It proved to be the start of something which lasted for over forty years; something that has given me even greater pleasure than cricket; that has made for me many more friends, and caused me more frustration than any other activity, in particular when, in the first year or so, I was bitten by the "golf bug", and was intent on becoming a very good player. However, like any other sport, it needs a tremendous amount of time and effort, and, unfortunately, I had so many other commitments that my ambition was a forlorn one. Nevertheless, to achieve a single-figure handicap, after starting so late in life, is not too bad an achievement.

For five years, I was fairly happy with my lot. I had a secure job, where I was making progress; I had a happy family life, with my three children – born in 1950, 1955 and 1958 – all thriving, and my wife settling into my new routine; she had ceased being a cricket widow, and was now a golf widow. However, one or two little niggles were developing at work. My new business figures were pretty good, and I welcomed the congratulations which came my way, but it soon became apparent that promotion was not really dependent upon one's selling ability alone. It was most important that one should keep in with one's superiors; to be at their beck and call; to join them in their frequent social drinking sessions; to generally kow-tow to them. In addition, when generous annual salary increases were announced, it apparently mattered not that one person had, maybe, put in many hours of extra work in the evenings and at weekends, to produce more business than other. All employees in a similar grade would receive the same increase.

I didn't think that this was right so in 1963 I was at the cross roads once more. I was determined to remove myself from my secure situation, and go it alone so that I could benefit from my efforts. I spoke at length with my father, but he felt that I was playing with fire and what I was proposing by going alone was fraught with danger. To give up a good job, plus its ancillary benefits; to put my wife and family at risk. To his way of thinking it was not at all sensible, but his way of thinking was not mine. After all, he was a splendid example of dedication and loyalty to one company. Starting as an office boy at the age of nineteen, he had stayed with one insurance company, at the same branch, until his retirement in 1960, by which time he had come up through the ranks and reached the top position of Branch Manager. Ironically had he stayed on a couple of years, and had I not made my decision to leave Northern Assurance Group, we may well have been working together, as his company and mine merged in the middle of the 1960s.

When I say that I wanted to go alone, this was not quite correct. I had the contacts and the experience, but no promises. The simple answer was to find someone who had, and in this I was fortunate. An old school friend provided accommodation above his shop in Cardiff, and we set up a partnership as insurance brokers. He was not knowledgeable in insurance matters, but looked after the books, and introduced business from his circle of friends. It was hard graft for a year of two, with not much to show for our efforts, but the fact that we were prepared to give a service to all and sundry, virtually at any time, paid dividends. Soon we were able to augment our staff, and in a most satisfactory way.

Since his retirement, I had noticed that my father was missing his previous routine, and that it was affecting his health adversely. He had always been an active man, not only in business, but also in pursuit of his love and knowledge of music. An expert organist; a fine tenor voice, coupled with an ability to conduct, had kept him busy, but the cessation of his business life left a large gap that needed to be filled. He duly came to work for me, albeit on a part-time basis, but the change in him was dramatic. He loved it, and of course, proved to be an invaluable asset with his tremendous experience.

The business grew to such an extent that I was highly delighted. The gamble had been taken, and had succeeded. Ultimately, we were approached by a large London-based Lloyds broking firm, looking for representation in Wales, and became the subject of a take-over. It seemed and ideal arrangement. I obtained a small amount of capital, plus the security of a service agreement and felt that my clients would benefit from the additional expertise of the Lloyds backers. I was wrong. There is no doubt in my mind now that the larger an organisation grows the less efficient it becomes, and the merger soon proved it. The handling of accounts, claims, etc was centralised in the London office, and most decisions on day-to-day working emanated from there as well.

The outcome was that the clients suffered; their accounts invariably were wrong; they became disgruntled; business was lost; targets were not reached, and heads started to roll – at least, that of my erstwhile partner. Another decision was required and I made it. I had proved that business was there to be picked up, and I knew I could handle it locally. I severed my connection with the London group; tore up my service agreement, and bought back my original company. I was still fairly well known in the area, and set up a new company, trading in my own name, starting again with the nucleus of my previous clientele.

Within a further five years, by dint of more hard effort, it had built up again, and I was able to provide for myself a good standard of living, but more particularly, the personal and local service that my clients required. Now there were further considerations. As the business grew, I found that I was putting in more and more hours, but at the same time I was reluctant to contemplate delegating the specialist work to others as I felt that the standard might be lowered.

In the hope that my eldest son, who was now twenty-five, would come into the firm, I had taken the first steps. He had graduated from university with a decent degree, and I had secured for him a position with an insurance company, thinking, as in my case, that a couple of year's good grounding would stand him in good stead. The other factor was that I had seen so many businessmen work hard up to the age of sixty five, then retire with the happy prospect of many years of enjoyment given to the pursuit of their favourite hobbies, only to die within a very short time *thereafter. For me, I had my goals; I longed to travel, and reside in the sun. If at all possible, I wanted to do this long before I was 65.*

Long-term planning is all very well, but it seldom comes to fruition. The first fly in the ointment was my son. After two years in insurance, he confessed to me that it wasn't in his blood, and that he did not wish to continue it. There was nothing I could say or do about it, because he was reacting much the same as I had done all those years before when my father had first put the suggestion to me. After much soul-searching, a possible solution came to me. I would look for another benefactor to take over my company, but this time it would have to be a local firm, not a London-based one, and I would wish to retain an interest. A few words in the right direction, and contact was made.

The outcome was an arrangement whereby a proportion of my shares were sold, for which I received a capital payment; also the remainder of my shares, plus a three-year service agreement, at the end of which time, if I so desired, the new controllers would purchase these shares at an agreed figure, leaving me free to retire and live on capital investment, or remain as a non-executive Director on a consultancy basis. A suitable arrangement, indeed, as by that time I would be 55, and the age at which I had decided to ease back in order to pursue my many other leisure interests.

15

MALLORCA TRAVEL

Leisure habits started to change in Britain during the 1950s, initially with families being attracted to the holiday experience at the new caravan parks or Butlin-style holiday camps. There was also the start of a trend for overseas holidays, and as a result, those people who previously might have gone to traditional British resorts such as Scarborough or Blackpool with their family during the inter-war period were now venturing *en famille* to somewhat more exotic locations nearer the shores of the Mediterranean.

It had a knock-on effect on cricket as these trips across the English Channel may have improved the children's grasp of the French language, but the flip-side was that it meant many young boys learnt new leisure patterns during the summer months, rather than watching and idolising the likes of cricketing stars such as Jack Hobbs, Wally Hammond or Frank Woolley as their father's had done at an early age. And when these young boys subsequently became fathers themselves, they continued the trend during the 1970s and 1980s for a summer exodus abroad to the package holiday capitals on the Costa del Sol, the Algarve, the Greek Islands or in Florida.

As personal transport improved and flights abroad became commonplace, a greater range of holiday destinations opened up. At the same time, there was a boom in other types of recreation as tennis, golf, badminton and squash came within the reach of more and more people. Whereas once there was the prospect of football in the winter, cricket in the summer, and an evening at the dance hall or cinema – as Jim had experienced throughout most of his career as a professional sportsman – there was now a far wider choice. With more recreational possibilities, it meant that fewer people were catching the cricket bug, despite a steady rise in the U.K. population and the post-war baby boom.

These new leisure habits and pastimes were also fuelled by the images now seen daily on the television set, and with greater personal mobility, cars opened up new avenues for people to follow at home when seeking healthy recreation, whilst the advent of package flights to the European landmass, opened up the prospect of continental holidays for relatively comfortably off people such as Jim.

My own desire to travel probably stemmed from my wartime journeys which, although undertaken at His Majesty's expense in cramped conditions, and always subject to strict discipline, endeared me to the type of climates available elsewhere. What a change from the grey skies, frequent rain, and muddy waters of Britain to be able to bask in unbroken sunshine, and to bathe in warm, crystal clear seas.

My short glimpse of the Mediterranean had not been enough, and I was determined to find a way of spending much more time in that area. The package style holidays had begun, and I arranged a two-week holiday in Majorca, despite the fact that my only other experience of aircraft had been a ten-minute flight from Cardiff to Weston-super-Mare and back, when the whole of the Glamorgan team plus baggage were piled into a single engine propeller type plane to suffer a hair-raising journey.

I had heard good reports of the island of Majorca, its sun, and its cheapness. It was fortunate that I picked on the resort of Cala Millor, situated on the east coast, about forty miles from the capital city of Palma. The area was unspoilt, despite the presence of many multi-storey hotels in the resort itself, and to my delight, my wife, two younger children and I at once loved the warmth, the peacefulness and the easy going way of life. It was a far cry from the pressures of professional sport and business, and if ever there were a place where I should be content to spend most of my remaining life, this was it.

The tours around the island were well organised, and in addition to the modern comfortable hotels – with their plentiful and varied menus plus decent recreational facilities – there were guided tours to caves, safari parks, markets, pearl, leather and glass factories, the whole being rounded off by late-night barbecues, where great portions of chicken, suckling pig, and vegetables were heaped onto one's plate, and washed down by copious quantities of the local wine or sangria. It was an excellent way of travelling around the island, and seeing its great natural beauty. The rest of the time we spent swimming, sun-bathing, shopping, riding in donkey carts, and even cycling, with bicycles being readily available for hire at ridiculously low prices.

For three or four years we were easily lured back for our annual summer holiday, and on one occasion even for a week in January, when we were astonished to find the temperature in the seventies, with scarcely a cloud in the sky. The cost of return flight plus full board was only twenty five pounds. On later visits, having sampled all the available day tours, we tended to make our way about to our favourite spots, one of which was the attractive, unspoiled resort of Porto Cristo, situated about five miles south of Cala Millor. We had passed through it before in order to visit the marvellous Cuevas Del Drach (Caves of the Dragon), which attracted thousands of tourists through the year.

One day my wife and I caught the local bus from Cala Millor to Porto Cristo. After sampling the delights of a lovely sandy beach, we decided to look for a mid-day snack. A nearby supermarket attracted our attention, and we entered to make our purchases. At the check-out till was a small chubby Mallorquin man, and I hastily turned to my Spanish phrase book in order to make suitable conversation. I uttered a couple of short sentences in halting, and far from correct Spanish, and duly waited for his reaction. It came in the form of a huge grin, as he said, "Perhaps it would be better if we spoke in English". It transpired that Pepe, as I came to know him, had been born in Felanitx, some twenty miles South of Porto Cristo, and, quite apart from his English, was a pretty good linguist in German, French, Dutch, Danish, plus his mother tongues of Spanish and Mallorquin. It was the beginning of a friendship that lasted for many years. Pepe, apparently, had learned his languages while working in a restaurant in Palma, and my next question was an obvious one. Why had he left a job like that to work in a supermarket in a small town over thirty miles away?

It was an interesting story. In the course of his work in the restaurant, he naturally came into contact with people of all creeds, colours, shapes and sizes. Those he saw regularly became friends as well as patrons, in particular a middle-aged British couple who had retired to the island. In time, Dorothy and her husband came to regard Pepe almost as a son. Then the husband died, leaving Dorothy a little capital; she heard of the opportunity of opening a shop in the Porto Cristo area, and persuaded Pepe to run it for her. Dorothy, a much travelled lady from Dorset, acquired an apartment near the shop, and the British/Mallorguin partnership prospered.

Our friendship with, firstly, Pepe, and later Dorothy, developed to such an extent that, instead of having to accept the package tour type of hotel, with its attendant regimentation, we were able to take advantage of the kind invitation to stay with them, the apartment being large enough to accommodate us. In addition, there were occasions when they were able to find a vacant villa for us, which made for a very different holiday during which we could eat, sleep and generally take our leisure as and when we wanted.

Pepe was an extremely hard worker. The roles of manager, buyer, delivery man, clerk, and cashier all came alike to him, and there were never any worries about clock-watching with Pepe's routine being as follows – up each morning at six; in the local market at seven, buying fresh bread and vegetables; back to open the shop. A short afternoon siesta break from 1.30pm to 3.30pm, and then working straight through until eight o'clock in the winter and ten or eleven o'clock in the summer. He had no thought of taking holidays himself, except on the saints days, and Bank Holidays, when closing was compulsory anyway, but one year we did persuade him to take a couple of weeks in February, and he came over to stay with us in Cardiff. His holiday coincided with a fall of snow, which he had never seen before at close range, and his delight was infectious. He lost no time in committing it all to film, and was rarely without his camera. The visit was partly educational, as he acquired a new language – Welsh. Well, at least we taught him the few phrases we knew!

Porto Cristo had everything we wanted, and we asked our friends to tell us immediately if they ever heard of an apartment becoming vacant. One day Dorothy said; "by the way, I believe that Louise (an English widow) is going back to England *permanently, and that her apartment ......" Before she could finish speaking, I pushed Dorothy into Pepe's car, and away we went. From the outside the property looked neat, compact, modern, and imposing, and outer coating of pink just providing the final attractive effect. It was the first floor apartment, with one below and one above, the building being detached, and on a corner facing two roads at right angles to each other. It was just up the hill from the beach, not more than a two minute walk.*

We knocked at the apartment door; the occupant was in, and was glad to show us around. The interior was even more charming; a central hall way with three bedrooms, a lounge, dining room, bathroom and kitchen leading off. All the floors were beautifully tiled; the kitchen contained a double drainer sink unit, fitted tables and cupboards, plus a refrigerator, and the woman's touch was evident from the flowers, neat pelmets and curtains, and general air of being lived-in. We went back for my wife. She saw it; she loved it. Could we have it? We could, and we did. How fortunate that I had been able to manage my affairs at home so that I had ample time to enjoy it for many years afterwards, when we spent a couple of months in the spring and a couple in the autumn savouring the delights of the Island. I was a lucky man indeed!

16

GOLF

Many county cricketers are decent golfers. During Jim's time as a professional sportsman, golf was one of the preferred activities on Sundays. The same is still true today, with the Professional Cricketers Association having their own tournament, whilst county cricketers and umpires are often involved in pro-am tournaments, corporate events and other functions – often as part of a Benefit Year – on the local golf courses.

Some Glamorgan cricketers have also been talented golfers, with Tom Barlow who played for the Welsh county between 1894 and 1897 being Welsh Amateur champion in 1900. However, the most famous golfer to appear for Glamorgan CCC was probably Tony Duncan who played twice for Glamorgan in 1934 whilst an undergraduate at Oxford University. The right-handed batsman subsequently played for Oxford University in 1935, before becoming one of the leading British amateur golfers either side of the Second World War, playing in the Walker Cup, and winning the Welsh Amateur Championships on four occasions between 1938 and 1954. Tony and his family also became leading figures with the Royal Porthcawl club, winning numerous tournaments and prizes.

Jim was not quite in Tony's league with a set of golf clubs in hand but even so, like countless other cricketers and sporting men and women, he thoroughly enjoyed a round of golf.

I had first taken up golf in 1958 and soon found that the camaraderie which exists in all good golf clubs knows no bounds, and the relationships which are consequently build up, I found to be far more lasting than those in other sports. Year in and year out the same four people can be seen playing together, apparently never tiring of each other's company; taking golfing and family holidays together; meeting together socially two or three times a week.

In my case, the very first year I joined my Club in Llanishen saw the commencement of such a relationship with three companions of varying circumstances and temperament. Two of them were twenty years older than I; the other six years older. Their occupations were, respectively, the Managing Director of a paint firm; the Branch Manager of an insurance company, and an Area Representative of a gas appliance firm. They were all married with families, but in only one other respect were there similarities. Each one of us played to win in a hard and uncompromising manner. No quarter was given or asked for. We thus became the founder members of a flourishing golf society within a golf club, and did not have to dwell too long when seeking a suitable name. The vulture being an uncompromising bird of prey it was ideally suited to our type of play, and the "Vultures" we

Jim learns the rudiments of golf with his mother in the early 1930s.

became for the next twenty years, playing as a group in many parts of Britain, in France, and in Portugal.

Very early on came my own initiation, when having missed a hole-able putt, I casually picked up my ball, which had come to rest no more than a couple of inches from the hole, assuming that it would automatically be given to me. I realised my mistake when a duet emanated from the opposition; "who gave you that?" No one had, of course, and they promptly claimed the hole. If, when teeing up the ball, I happened to stray an inch or so in front of the marker boxes, my opponents would say nothing until my drive had split the fairway two hundred yards ahead, then again would give voice together: "go and get it and play it again, old chap, from the proper position". If there was any question as to whose ball lay further from the hole on the putting surface, and, therefore, had to be played first, it was not sufficient for one of us to say: "you to play". More often than not it would end up with the four of us pacing out the respective distances to verify who was to play; sometimes even the flagstick would be employed, as a measuring device if the pacing left any reasonable, or unreasonable, doubt.

When we were considering our first annual golfing trip, the fact that I had spent most of the summers travelling around the country was immensely helpful, and, at my suggestion, we decided eventually to settle for the New Forest area in the vicinity of Christchurch from which the courses at Ferndown, Parkstone, and Brockenhurst were within easy reach. These golfing weeks were quite physically demanding as we played two hundred and thirty four holes during our stay. It did miracles for my game and after returning home weary but happy, I would stand on the first tee of my local and very short, course, confident in the knowledge that it presented no terrors. Invariably my initial tee shot would be a wild slice with the ball disappearing into an out-of-bounds field, never to be seen again!

Jim on the golf course in the late 1970s.

Word of our exploits quickly spread through our own golf club, and other members expressed an interest in the possibility of joining the Vultures. As a result, the original four became eight, then twelve. During the subsequent years trophies were donated and played for; social functions, with and without wives, materialised, and long-standing friendships were formed. Off the course we were bosom pals, but when on it you could be excused for thinking we were sworn enemies, frequently engaging in much verbal abuse if one thought that maybe the other had gained an unfair advantage by dubious methods. But the affection in which everyone was held was evidenced by the presentation of a seat, in memory of deceased members, which was placed in a prominent position near the first tee of our club.

One year, when Wales played France in the Five Nations Rugby Championship in Paris, four of us decided to have the best of both worlds by travelling to France in two cars, finding a golf course on which to play, and then, on the Saturday, head to Paris to see the match. It proved to be an excellent decision. The journey was uneventful, and we found a good hotel in Chantilly, twenty miles from Paris, and near a superb golf course.

After arriving on the Friday, I was deputed to see the Secretary of the Chantilly course and make arrangements for our round of golf. To my delight, he swiftly put paid to my halting French by replying in a broad Scots accent and in no time had organised a game as well as lunch and dinner. Although Wales lost the match, the trip had been so successful, we decided to repeat the venture whenever Wales met France in Paris, and to keep the peace, we also included our wives on these cross-Channel visits!

Despite copious pre-planning, some of these ventures across to France were quite eventful, such as the time where a variety of difficulties with our cars led us one snowy February to nearly miss our ferry from the South Coast to Le Havre. Thanks to the assistance of the RAC, we made it to Southampton in sufficient time, but on arriving in Northern France, we encountered a severe snow storm, ruling out any golfing activity. There were doubts as well about the rugby international taking place, but it got the green light and we hastily made our way by train to the Gare Du Nord and joined the throng of people entering the Stadium. Despite wearing pyjamas, a suit, two sweaters, two pairs of socks and a thick overcoat, the cold still got through, and the apathetic performance of the Welsh team, far more outclassed that the score-line suggested, did nothing to warm our enthusiasm. We did not hang around for very long after the final whistle and soon headed back into Paris to meet the ladies, before returning to have dinner in Chantilly and our return crossing, with all concerned – and their teeth still chattering – wondering who had had the temerity to suggest a sporting long weekend in Paris in the middle of one of the hardest winters for sixteen years!

Another ambitious, but much warmer golfing trip was to Estoril, some fifteen miles outside Lisbon, in Portugal. Again it involved a morning cross-channel journey from Southampton, followed by overnight stops at Royan and San Sebastian. At Estoril, where Kings and Princes resided, and patronised the famous casino, we stayed in the magnificent five-star Palaccio Hotel. A superb bedroom suite for each husband and wife, with private bathroom, and full board, cost the equivalent of only four pounds per day per person, and the service was incredibly good. Lording it over the huge dining room, catering for a hundred guests as cosmopolitan as the Headquarters of the United Nations, was a head waiter par excellence. He had the ability to recognize the nationality of every person who entered that room, and to greet them in their own tongue. We thought we had him when he greeted us in English, and we told him we were Welsh, had he ever heard of us? "Please wait a moment", he requested; disappeared from the room, and returned with a sheet of music. It was "Ar Hyd Y Nos" (All Through the Night), in Welsh and we were flabbergasted. "It so happens", he said, "that I spent a few months in the Seabank Hotel in Porthcawl in your delightful country".

We had plenty of adventures on our home courses, including Barton-on-Sea, between Bournemouth and Lymington, which is a fascinating little course. Mind you, they have their problems, in particular with the first two holes, which run parallel to, and right alongside, the cliff edge. The tees and greens of these holes are literally within feet of the fifty feet drop down to the beach below. One problem is erosion; the sea encroaches every year, and by undercutting the cliff, washes away a foot or so of the cliff in the process. The result is that the tees have to be moved further and further inland, while the greens get smaller. The other problem is the wind. It is always there, and no one seems to know just which way it is going to blow. A screamer of a drive hit straight down the middle can fly into wind, deviate rapidly, and disappear over the cliff – not the sort of start one wants in a medal competition!

Over the years, caution had become the watch-word, and everyone tended to play from the tee at an angle of forty five degrees to the left, away from the cliff. This is all very well, except that it can be a dangerous practice, because the poor chaps putting on the eleventh green are right in the firing line. The solution was to erect a high wire screen of mesh, extending to a height of about fifteen feet to the left of the first tee, and about thirty yards from the cliff edge.

The first time we played the course, another of our founder members drove off to the left, playing safe, and created a further interesting problem. The ball went rather higher that required, struck the top of the mesh screen, and lodged itself firmly a few inches from the top. Our colleague was non-plussed, and turned to me, his opponent, for guidance. What was he to do? "No problem", I said, "you must play it as it lies". The sequel was quite amusing; to reach the ball he was obliged to stand on the shoulders of his partner; hold his three iron at full stretch in his right hand, and give it a whack, He did, and made beautiful contact. The ball flew out at a rate of knots, bounced twice, and disappeared over the edge of the cliff, never to be seen again. The moment was recorded for posterity on our small cine camera, and if ever we want to brighten long winter evenings it would get a ready airing.

We always enjoyed playing at the beautiful course at Brockenhurst Manor, in the very heart of the New Forest, and again it holds special memories for me in particular. As a county cricketer aims for the maiden hundred or five-wicket haul, so must every golfer, whether he is a professional or a twenty-four handicap hacker, aims for that which brings the greatest thrill of all – a hole in one. For me, it happened at Brockenhurst on a lovely summer morning one June. The twelfth hole is a par three off one hundred and sixty yards, with all sorts of trouble between tee and green, and a deep wood on the left hand side. There was a slight breeze blowing against us, and, preferring to be long rather than short, I selected a four wood. The shot was not very well executed, and the ball went off the heel of the club straight at the woods on the left. A cry of glee; "it's in the forest", from our opponents, was quickly stifled, as they watched the ball strike the top of the tree, deflect to the right, drop onto the green and disappear into the hole. One of them at least had the courtesy to pick it out for me. It proved to be the first of five holes-in-one I achieved, and I am glad to record that the others were obtained, without any luck, and with far more orthodox methods.

17

A RETURN TO COUNTY CRICKET

The 1960s were a successful decade for Glamorgan CCC, with back-to-back victories over the 1964 and 1968 Australians, as well as a second county title, under the captaincy of Tony Lewis in 1969. The decade also saw Peter Walker and Jeff Jones play with distinction for England, whilst two other legendary Glamorgan players – Alan Jones and Don Shepherd – established themselves as the finest opening batsman and off-cutter respectively in county cricket.

But behind the scenes it was not all sweetness and light in the affairs of the Welsh county as, not for the first time, Wilf Wooller was embroiled in several heated debates with other Club officials and committee members. Wilf had retired from playing in 1960 to become the Club's Secretary, but in the same way that he had been a hard and dogmatic captain on the field, he was a forthright and outspoken individual in the committee room. It led to a series of resignations from the committee, and with vacancies up for grabs, Jim was one of the new faces to assist with the Club's administration as – after a ten year break from the county game – he was appointed onto the county's committee

Glamorgan CCC had been going through a rather traumatic period in its history, with the Committee becoming divided over certain issues. Again, Wilf Wooller was in the middle of it, and the committee were split in two. The outcome was that Wilf continued in his capacity of Secretary; many of the Committee members resigned, and a new Committee was formulated. I was approached to stand as it was felt that I, with my past background as a player and someone who had taken the field alongside Wilf, had something to offer. I duly allowed my name to go forward and was pleased to be elected.

It was felt that my own particular forte lay in the cricketing rather than the administration side; having been a professional, I knew the thoughts of the players; their problems, and their needs. Despite the generation gap, it seemed to work, and, over the years that followed, it became a labour of love, attending meetings, travelling with the team, negotiating contracts, and, in the process, meeting many old friends and adversaries. Wherever I went, there would be someone I had not seen for ten

The Glamorgan side at The Oval in 1963. Standing: AHM Rees, DGL Evans, IJ Jones, PM Walker, EJ Lewis and A Jones. Seated: JS Pressdee, DJ Shepherd, OS Wheatley, BL Muncer and B Hedges.

or twenty years acting in a similar capacity for another county; or as a coach, or even standing as umpire. Old memories would come flooding back, and many an hour was spent in discussing the merits and demerits of the personalities of our era. The grounds where I had experienced elation or despair were the same; so were the dressing rooms. It was as if I had been able to put the clock back.

My duties as a committee member were many and varied, including attending dinners arranged by local amateur clubs at which the organisers required the presence of a professional or ex-professional to earn his free meal by talking about the game, and his own experiences, for anything up to an hour, and, afterwards answering the many questions both from the knowledgeable and the other kind. Lunches, too, were sometimes offered by such as the Rotary Clubs, and, while they were of necessity much shorter affairs, with members requiring to return to their places of business, the occasions were very pleasurable.

I also had a stint as Match Manager at the various one-day games which Glamorgan staged at home and which were added to the county calendar from the 1960s onwards. I largely oversaw the matches at Cardiff, and occasionally at Swansea, with my duties including making some announcements over the tannoy and liaising with sponsors over the adjudication and awarding of Man-of-the-Match medals. Knowing more than a bit about what was going on out in the middle helped both of these duties and although I had no experience of playing in these limited overs contests, there were rarely any issues or controversies.

Indeed, it was Wilf whose announcements had irked a few people in Championship matches, especially in the early 1970s, including at a game in Swansea when

Gilbert Parkhouse, Trevor Bailey, Bill Edwards and Tony Lewis.

he became so irate at what he perceived to be the negative tactics of the visiting captain by blocking and blocking for over after over, rather than trying to go for runs and set a target, that he announced over the public address system at the St. Helen's ground that if anyone wanted their admission money refunded they should see him in the Pavilion!

Being on the Glamorgan committee also allowed me to watch my first-ever Test Match between England and Pakistan in 1972/73– in Pakistan! The chance to travel to an overseas Test came completely out of the blue and followed a phone call from Bill Edwards, another Glamorgan Committee member. Through his sports shop at Swansea, he was providing kit and equipment for many Test teams, and had developed a connection with Pakistan International Airlines, who had promised Bill a return flight to Karachi at nominal cost for up to three people. Would I like to be one of them? Of course I would: It was a very special occasion anyway, and likely to make history, as Glamorgan had two players involved; on opposite sides, and both Captains at that. Tony Lewis for England, and Majid Khan for Pakistan. It was too good an opportunity to miss.

Accordingly, after hurried visits for vaccination and other purposes, I presented myself at Heathrow on the last day of February 1973, linked up with my two colleagues, and boarded flight PK701 to Karachi. Apart from package holiday trips, it was to be my first flight of any distance, and this distance was thousands of miles. The green and white Boeing 707 took off at 10am, flew smoothly over Munich and the Alps, and in four and a half hours was touching down at Damascus, where we were reminded to advance our watches by two hours.

We were soon airborne again for the one and a half hours flight to Baghdad, *where, after a short break, we set off on the final leg of three hours. It was 2am local time on St. David's Day (1st March) when we finally arrived in Pakistan, and our thoughts turned to baths, accommodation, food and flights to Lahore. Initially, the general idea was to travel from Karachi to Lahore by road, taking our time, and having a good look at the country on the way. However, we were soon disillusioned – apparently the distance was eight hundred miles, mostly over a vast desert, and the journey could take days. It was obvious that we should have to go by air, but, when due enquiries were made, there seemed little chance, as the one flight that day was fully booked.*

Nevertheless, Bill was equal to the occasion and he told the airline officials that we were delayed members of the England party, and that it was imperative that we arrive in time for the match. His ploy worked, and we were given first-class seats on the 7am flight to Lahore. There was just time for a quick bath; a snack, and a couple of hours' sleep, before we were on our way again.

Despite over-shooting the runway at Lahore and having to come into land for a second time, the journey was a pleasant one, taking no more than eighty minutes. The morning was beautifully warm and sunny, and we lost no time in taking a taxi to the Test Match stadium, where we hoped to arrange match tickets and accommodation, but we were unlucky this time; there was no one available to help us. No officials, and no cricketers. However, we did obtain Majid's home telephone number, and on ringing found that the teams were practising at the local Gymkhana Club, to where we immediately headed.

All was well once more; Majid took us in hand, insisted that we should stay at his home, and after practice, duly escorted us there, introducing us to his wife, two sisters, and his famous father, Jahangir Khan, who had played in the same Cambridge side as Wilf Wooller, and, later, for India before the Partition. He was also famous for the much-quoted incident at Lords, on which occasion he bowled a ball which unfortunately killed a swallow in flight, and whose body is preserved for posterity in the cricket museum at Lord's.

An empty house on the Khan estate, standing in magnificent grounds, was put at our disposal, and we took our meals with the family, which included Uncle Raza Khan, whom I had met fifteen years before. He was a prominent Government Official, and in 1958 had come to Cardiff to study Local Government for a year. Being a cricket fanatic, and a useful player at that, he guested for Cardiff CC and played when I was skipper, so we welcomed the opportunity to reminisce. Raza took charge of me in particular for the whole week of our stay, and his hospitality was overwhelming.

Jahangir Khan himself was tall, stately, well-mannered and beautifully dressed in British-style clothes. Like Majid he was a highly articulate man also made us doubly welcome, and took delight in escorting us to the famous fort, mosques, gardens and tombs which dominated the City. We walked for hours, following his untiring steps, and returned absolutely worn out. We recovered in time for dinner, which was a magnificent affair; the table groaned with meat, rice, chicken and vegetable dishes, brought in by the numerous servants, and we needed no invitation to commence eating, although we were rather astonished when the ladies of the household did not join us. We soon learned that it was the custom for them to sit and eat only after the men had had sufficient (and had left something for them!) After such an eventful day, sleep was not difficult to come by.

Friday was the first day of the Test Match, and like so many days on the sub-Continent it dawned warm and sunny, and, after breakfast, we were whisked to the stadium by Raza Khan in his chauffeur driven limousine in time for the 10am start. Seated on the roof of the pavilion, the view was tremendous, surrounded by sixty thousand noisy and colourful people, who were not averse to enjoying a little light relief, if the cricket was dull, by lighting newspapers and throwing them on the

Majid Khan

pitch. Lunch was at noon, and Raza was not content to sample the available picnic hampers. Off we went with him to the sumptuously new Gymkhana Club, which had cost about £150,000 to build, the whole sum being subscribed by donations from the members.

At the tea interval, taken at 2.45pm, Raza had another bright idea. "That's enough cricket for today; we shall go and play golf". And he and I did just that. This pattern persisted for the remaining days of the match, except for one, which rather astonished my travelling companions, but which I thoroughly enjoyed.

On the Saturday evening, we were invited to the special dinner given by the Pakistan Board of Control at the Intercontinental Hotel, where the English Team were staying, and had the opportunity before the function of visiting the Team's suite to drink their health in private. Private it had to be, because it was the aftermath of the various terrorist activities, such as those which had tragically marred the Munich Olympics in 1972. Consequently, the England party were more or less confined to their quarters on the fifth floor of the hotel, the entrances to which were guarded by bearded warriors armed with loaded machine guns.

Sunday was another lovely day. After breakfast at the Khan house, we were again picked up by Raza and taken to the Gaddafi Stadium for the third day of the match. We settled for a picnic lunch on the ground, and for once decided to forego the golf and see a full day's play.

In the early evening we were guests at a cocktail party given by the British Consulate, whose gardens were superbly enhanced by a multi-coloured marquee, the whole being lit by fairy lights. It was a magnificent setting, and our welcome was a warm one, in particular as both the Consul, Mr. Morris and the Commercial Relations Officer, Mr. Jenkins, were fellow Welshmen.

Monday was a rest day as far as the Test was concerned, but not for us. Majid took us to his old school, Aitchinson College, situated just behind his house. It consisted of a marvellous collection of buildings standing in one hundred and seventy acres of grounds. We were first introduced to the Principal, then were privileged to join the assembly on the lawns outside; over one thousand pupils ranging from five to nineteen years of age, all dressed in blue, with highly starched turbans, and their teachers , including four from Britain. Prayers were said; a reading from the Koran given; the school song was sung, and Majid, a hero to them all, was introduced. For once in his life he was unable to avoid making a speech, and ended up by presenting an award to a twelve year old tennis player who was ranked number three in the country, and who had recently beaten numbers one and two.

All this was tending to show us the tremendous advantages enjoyed by the privileged few, and the vast difference between them and the millions of other inhabitants of Pakistan, who were living in squalor and poverty. The crippled beggars, shuffling along the dirty streets of Lahore, had, and would have, no future in this life, and merely emphasised the vast gulf between the haves and the have-nots in this less economically developed nation.

The Khan estate of a dozen or more beautiful houses, in its own little colony at Zaman Park, was in a completely different world. Thirty or forty of the Khans lived there, and so obviously intended to preserve their way of life and their opulence that they retained the practice of

Tony Lewis and Majid Khan at the toss in Karachi in 1973.

inter-marriage. Majid himself was

subject to this rule, and the bride chosen for him was his first cousin. However, in the event he was fortunate, because his wife Seema proved to be a highly intelligent and attractive girl who had spent many years in Sweden, where her father had been the Pakistan Ambassador.

On this particular Monday we received guided tours from three different Khan's. After being conducted by Majid around his marvellous school, Raza took us twenty miles out of Lahore into the countryside where was situated his farm, and we spent an interesting hour viewing the growing and cutting of the main crop – sugar cane. Majid's father, Jahangir, then took his turn in the afternoon, when he showed us the famous Shalimar Gardens, which had much in common with the Taj Mahal by reason of the fact that they had both been designed and constructed by the same man.

The next highlight was a visit to the old City of Lahore, which bore absolutely no resemblance to the modern, concrete, asphalt, and mechanical vehicle environment that lay just outside the still-standing ancient walls of the original City. It was like going into another world, with its congested, narrow streets and market stalls, all thronged with people dressed in the garb of the East which had stood the test of time. Jahangir admitted that he had not been in there for the past thirty five years, and yet, before we had gone a hundred yards, people were turning to stare at him, talking excitedly among themselves. They had recognised him for the great personality and cricketer that he had been.

It was the most hectic day of our visit, and we were glad to learn that the evening was to be a quiet one, with us joining the family at their private dinner party, held in Majid's house. Apart from Majid and his wife Seema, there were his mother and father; Raza Khan and his wife; Majid's two sisters, Sara and Shazi, and Shazi's husband Farouk, who was Raza Khan's son, thus further proving the trend for inter-marriage.

The next day was Tuesday, and our last in Pakistan – at least, as far as we knew, because, although we were due to fly out of Karachi that evening, the remainder of the trip was anything but certain. Leaving the Khan residence that morning after breakfast, we had time to spend with the members of the local infant's school for the simple reason that they were seated on the lawn in front of the house. Given the usually fine weather in Pakistan, the lawn was their normal place of learning, where they spent several hours of each week-day morning improving their knowledge. Of course, one of the subjects was English, it being the second language of the country.

Off we went to the Test Match again, which was turning out to be something of a stalemate, and, in the afternoon, I had my final game of golf with Raza. This time we also had the company of a Mr Cornelius, who, in addition to being the Chief Justice, was well-known as a former tour manager of the Pakistan Eaglets, a side of young cricketers which came to the U.K. to improve their game, and also caused *consternation by beating several county sides. The Eaglets had played various matches during the 1950s in South Wales against the Glamorgan 2nd XI and other scratch sides, so we had plenty to talk about as we made our way around the beautifully manicured course.*

Our farewell dinner was at Majid's but he himself was laid low with a viral infection. We left his bedside at 9pm in time to catch the evening flight to Karachi, but, on arrival at the airport, found that our Boeing 720 would be two hours late taking off. Eventually, it left at 11.45pm, and we touched down in Karachi at fifteen minutes after midnight. We were lucky again! A few hours' rest at the Midway Hotel, and we managed to book a flight on a Boeing 707 operating between Peking and New York, which left Karachi at 7am.

Three hours later we were in Teheran, trying to become acclimatized to a temperature of 48 degrees Fahrenheit, which naturally contrasted greatly with the 85 degrees, experienced in Karachi. The next leg of our journey was on to Beirut, where, after a two and a half hour journey, we made an instrument landing in heavy rain. Up again, and another two and a half hours of travel brought us to Athens, which looked marvellous on approach. A sunny 60 degrees, and beautifully calm, it looked both clean and fresh, and an ideal place for a holiday. A final stop at Geneva, and we were soon touching down at Heathrow, by which time tiredness had set in; not surprising, considering that the journey from Lahore had taken twenty-four hours, with little or no sleep being possible, mainly because of a tummy bug due most likely to the exotic food and not-too-clean water we had encountered. Still, it proved to be a fascinating experience.

18

RETIREMENT IN THE SUN

With an ageing population and a falling birth rate in Britain, the question of raising the retirement age has become a political issue for governments of all hue and colour during recent years. In some cases, it's been a quite sensitive one as people continue working on beyond the traditional retirement ages of 65 for men and 60 for women. Jim though hailed from a different generation where these dates were set in tablets of stone. If you were careful in managing your income and personal finances, an early retirement was also possible. This is what happened to Jim and to his delight he was able to spend plenty of time with his wife and family in their apartment in Mallorca.

For several years I had been planning for early retirement. When it came to fruition, my company became absorbed into a newly-formed insurance broking group; the remainder of my shares were purchased; I was retained as a non-Executive Director with no fixed duties, and my time was my own. I was now able to spend several months of the year with my wife at our Mallorca apartment; come home for my summer of cricket and golf, and, of course, to spend Christmas in Wales with the family gathered around.

As soon as I was a free agent, I decided to experiment with driving to Southern Spain thereby avoiding the tedium of airport delays and many boring and uncomfortable hours in over-heated departure lounges so we planned a route to Barcelona where we could join the luxury car ferry to Palma, arriving at 8pm. This left us only a fifty-minute drive to our apartment, and all involved a drive of 1150 miles in comfort from Cardiff to Porto Cristo. There were a few glitches on occasion, including the time when gales in the English Channel resulted in the ferry being cancelled and together with my wife – who is far from being the safest of sailors having to endure a hovercraft ride with more ups and downs than a Blackpool rollercoaster.

Whilst in Mallorca I developed a passion for fishing. There being no tide in the Mediterranean, the common British practice of digging for bait was not possible, so it was necessary to resort to the use of frozen shrimps, cheese, bread and anything else which the fish might find an attraction. The thrill of that first bite, and of actually landing a tiddler compared favourably with a superb iron shot biting back from the green and landing near the pin, or with a diving catch in the covers off a full-blooded stroke by a batsman. Mind you, the occasional success after many hours of fishing was not enough, and proved the need for better techniques, which led to the seeking of further information from the locals. The one thing they would not disclose was the composition of the paste-like bait, which was remarkably successful but, at least, I was able to find out about worms.

It appeared that these were imported from the mainland at weekends, and that, if kept in sawdust, they would stay alive for two or three days. The purchase of these meant success on Saturday, Sunday, and possibly Monday, but even these catches were no more than a few inches long. Not having a boat was a handicap, and restricted me to fishing from rocks, piers and harbours, but one day I noticed some tourists idly throwing pieced of bread on the surface of the water. Immediately, the bread was surrounded by dozens of small, and later, larger fish, biting chunks out of it until it had all disappeared. Here, it seemed, was the ideal bait.

The next essential was a suitable current or back-wash to allow the floating bread to drift out from shore when cast, as the fish had a habit of gathering abut fifty metres off-shore, where the discharging sewage would reach them. On this, my first occasion, all seemed to be well, and the chunk of bread, with its trailing float, drifted slowly out to where the fish waited in their dozens. Suddenly they spotted it, and made a bee-line for this tasty morsel. Sure enough, before long, one had ventured too far; there was a mighty pull on the line, and I had him. Reeling the fish in carefully, I made one mistake; Fishing from the rocks, I was about fifteen feet above the water line, and, having pulled it in, the moment I took the strain and lifted it out, its weight was too much, and the hook became dislodged; it was lost, and I was sadder and wiser. Thereafter, whenever I caught one, and reeled it in, I contrived to manoeuvre it on a flat rock level with the water; made the line secure, and climbed down to complete the catch.

This method can be very frustrating if the wind is wrong; if the bread is not quite right; if the fish decide to wait for the sewage one hundred and ten metres out; if a school of small fish gobble up the bread before it has reached their big brothers; or if the fish, when trapped, takes the line under a sharp shelf of rock, and snaps it. But, if all is well, it is a tremendous thrill to hook a three or four-pounder, and bring it safely ashore – and then take it home – and to eat it.

The biggest catch I made also gave me the biggest surprise. It was a beautiful afternoon; no wind, and the sea was like a sheet of glass. My wife and I walked the hundred yards from our apartment to the rocks near the outlet, and I left her to sunbathe while I prepared for battle. Soon the bread bait was floating on the water some sixty yards out, and I sat back on a rock, waiting for the bait to be taken. It soon was, but not in the manner expected. A large gull, looking for fish, circled the water, spotted the bread, dived on it, picked it up, and flew off. At least, it tried to fly off, but only managed to rise about ten feet above the surface of the water. One triple hook had caught in its beak, and another in its leg; the combined weight of the line and the plastic float, which was still on the water, defeated its efforts to proceed further. Ultimately, after making frantic efforts to fly off, it gave up the struggle, and settled on the surface of the sea.

Without further ado, I decided to reel it in, and before long it was out of the water, looking bleakly but patiently at me. It was as big as a goose. I unhooked the float, and carried it, with the bird dangling from the end of the trace, up to where my wife was lolling peacefully in the sun. I said: "What do you think I have caught this time?" She looked; had the shock of her life, and burst into laughter. "It's your biggest yet", she commented. We had to try and remove the hooks, so she cradled the huge bird in her arms while I went to work with the pliers; the captive looked balefully at us; never uttered a sound, and did not move.

Eventually, I managed to get the hook out of its beak, where upon it promptly flapped its wings, bit my wife on her hand, and flew off at a great rate, with the other hooks, my trace, and plastic float, all hanging from its leg in such a way that it looked like a man being winched down from a helicopter. It soon disappeared, and we never saw it again!

Another time, there was a period of bad weather in Mallorca, with easterly winds blowing into my stretch of coast. Even in rough weather, provided that the bait is allowed to drift out, the fish will bite, but the easterlies meant that there was no chance of that. Just for something to do, I fished from a road bridge at the very innermost point of the harbour, where the water was only about two feet deep, and watched the tiny fishes eating the bread away, with no worries about being caught, as my hooks were too large.

Suddenly, there was a flurry in the water, the bread was taken, and something sizeable and strong was on the end of my line. In the next few minutes the fish dived

to the shallow bottom, managed to twist my line around the mooring rope of a small fishing boat, and left me hanging on grimly to the rod. I reeled in very slowly, expecting every moment that the line would break; but it held. There was one more thing I had to do. I jumped on board the fishing boat, passed my rod under the mooring rope to untwist the line; reeled in some more; leant over the side of the boat as the fish came to the surface, and grabbed it with my free left hand. It was

Early adventures with a boat! Jim and his parents in 1935.

a beautiful three-pounder; a brilliant yellow and white-striped local delicacy which had no business to be there, and known as a saupa. At the end, I was panting with effort, but it made my day, and my evening meal!

Anyone who has spent any length of time either in the sea or on it will realise the fascination it invokes. It's different moods, alternating between calm and peaceful benevolence to stormy, nasty viciousness, can do nothing to lessen this fascination; to be honest, if anything, it tends to add to it. I am a pretty good sailor, in that the most fearsome of seas, and its consequent effect upon a ship in which I might be travelling, although putting in my mind feelings of trepidation regarding my personal safety and that of others, does not have any physical effect on me.

The miserable and uncomfortable "Mal De Mer" does not attack me, and never has done, except once; The crossing from Southampton to Normandy on D Day minus 1, in gale conditions, was enough to make even seasoned sailors ill, the particular reason being that our small landing craft of only a few hundred tons was flat-bottomed, with the result that, in heavy seas, it behaved most oddly, and, apart from the usual pitch and roll, contrived a series of movements which I had never expected to encounter.

The fact that I love the water so much; the appearance of it; the sound of it, is all the more remarkable when one realises what a poor swimmer I am. Presumably, when I am in it, I have no confidence; when I am on it, I am exhilarated by it. When I am abroad, I spent hours every day wading in it, or fishing it. The only thing missing for me was some way of spending time on it, other than the sometimes boring car ferries which I was obliged to take.

I was fortunate therefore to purchase from a friend a small inflatable boat complete with a two horse-power motor. It opened up new horizons for me. The beauty of it was that it could be parcelled up so minutely as to fit comfortably into the back of the car, or even into the boot, Although there were numerous extras to be carried; floorboards, inflator, life jackets (very necessary for me) and inflatable seat. I soon became adept at packing, removing, inflating, deflating, and the many other tasks involved.

Fuel was no problem, although the tank would hold only about one litre. It was enough at three-quarters speed to give me about three hours' use of the engine at a cost of less than 50p. The fifty-to-one petrol/oil mixture was actually sold in the pumps by the local petrol stations, so the acquisition of a five litre can meant that I had plenty in reserve. So it was that, in the space of a couple of months, I had explored about fifteen miles of coast line; inlets, creeks, harbours, with little or no trouble. The acquisition of this inflatable made complete my Mallorcan adventures and whether fishing or sailing, I spent countless blissful hours under the Mediterranean sun.

Lucky Jim indeed!

19

THE CHANGING FACE OF COUNTY CRICKET

By the time Jim returned to Glamorgan CCC in the 1960s as a committee member, the county game had dramatically changed. No longer did the fixture calendar consist solely of three-day matches against other county sides, touring teams, Oxford or Cambridge University or other scratch elevens. From 1963 one-day matches had been added to jazz-up the schedules and to bring the public thronging back through the turnstiles after a prolonged period of falling attendances and negative attitudes by some county captains who seemed more content to draw a Championship match than to risk losing by setting a generous target.

The 1960s also saw an increase in the number of overseas players as Test match stars from abroad increasingly spent the entire English summer with a county side, and the prospect of watching this galaxy of international talent also gave gate figures a boost. Indeed, the financial aspects of the county game became more and more important during the course of the next twenty or thirty years as county cricket became more of a business. The county's off-field team were now tasked with attracting decent sponsorship as well as attracting new players, and nurturing home-grown talent.

Glamorgan CCC, despite their national identity and unique position as Wales' sole representative in the world of county cricket, was not immune to financial problems, and under the eagle eye of Secretary Wilf Wooller, the club continued to be run on a shoestring, from a rented second floor office in the heart of Cardiff's city centre.

Indeed, by the time Glamorgan clinched their second county title under Tony Lewis in 1969, the Club still did not own any property. Instead, they paid rent to the likes of Cardiff Athletic Club as well as Swansea Cricket and Football Club, for the privilege of playing county cricket at the Arms Park and St. Helen's, as well as the other clubs whose grounds they used in a bid to fly the flag for county cricket across Wales. The use of outgrounds therefore was an expensive business, and coupled with the other rising costs and expenditure involved in running county cricket during the 1960s and 1970s,

it was helpful for Glamorgan to have someone like Jim, with an experience of business and the financial world who could offer advice in the committee room when the agenda moved away from purely cricketing matters.

Wilf Wooller in the Glamorgan office in High Street, Cardiff in 1977.

When I changed my viewpoint from a professional cricketer to that of an administrator following my election onto the Glamorgan committee, it was an education to see the game from the other side of the fence. The running costs of a county cricket club ensured that the Finance Committee and Treasurers across the county all suffered from permanent headaches as they tried to make ends meet. Match expenses, travel and hotel costs; players' wages – all spiralled upwards. The bulk of the Club's income came from members' subscriptions, Test Match receipts, sponsorship, radio and television, and the like. In themselves they were insufficient to cover outgoings, which is why the County Supporters' Clubs, with their lotteries and other fund-raising schemes were so very necessary to the parent clubs. Without them, many would have been unable to continue.

There is another important factor in the wellbeing of a county cricket club. It must have success on the field, otherwise interest will sag, membership will drip away and gates will become almost non-existent. Those of us who were lucky enough to be involved in Glamorgan's Championship years of 1948, 1969 and 1997 remember the tremendous impact produced by our success on the general public. Membership soared, gates were marvellous and interest in county cricket in general, and Glamorgan in particular, was fiercely intense. It showed what appeared to be the Welsh temperament in its true light. Whether it be rugby, soccer or cricket, if the team were doing well, then the home supporters, as partisan as they come, would turn out in their thousands to give their noisy but fervent support to the "boys".

Lack of success brings little support and only problems. As a committeeman, I frequently became aware of the fickleness of the man-in-the-street support. If the side won a couple of games, I was button-holed by excited cricket lovers, who would say; "aren't we doing well!" On the other hand, a few defeats and the comment was: "What's wrong with your team?"

One problem is that no one really seems to know what are the required ingredients to guarantee success. In 1948 we were quite an average bunch of players, with no great stars in the side, but, invariably, two or three would come good with bat or ball in each innings; the

Majid Khan and Eifion Jones on the balcony at Sophia Gardens in 1969 after Glamorgan clinched the Championship title.

fielding would be superb, and, in Wilf Wooller, we had a captain with the ability to instil confidence into us by his personal example. He feared nothing and nobody, and insisted so often that we were better than any other team that we actually believed it – and prospered accordingly. If there was a need for someone to open the innings on a wicked, rain-affected pitch; if someone had to bowl for several long hours on a perfect wicket on a baking hot day; if a fielder had to stand at short-leg no more than a yard from the bat, Wilf would say: "I'll do it".

Apart from boosting our moral, there was no doubt that it had a completely opposite effect on the opposition. Since that time, no other Glamorgan captain has ever looked like being produced from the same mould, or has been able to exert a similar influence over his players. Tony Lewis had several years of success, culminating in the Championship win in 1969, but he will be the first to admit that it was mainly brought about by the fact that he was fortunate in

Tony Cordle and Malcolm Nash toast the crowd in front of the Sophia Gardens pavilion after Glamorgan's victory over Worcestershire to become the County Champions of 1969.

105

having a well-balanced and experienced side giving him 100% support. The pity was also that he was unable to carry on for a few more years, primarily because of long-standing injuries to his knees and shoulder.

At that time, I was deeply involved in matters of team selection and general welfare of the players, and it became obvious that, after the euphoria of 1969 and the next couple of years, the morale of the side, and, consequently, the team spirit, was disintegrating. Tony's nagging shoulder pains caused him to generally lose interest in playing and carrying out his other off-field duties so necessary to the well-being of a team. Even so, he was on the verge of being picked as captain of the England side, and, indeed, skippered the MCC party on the 1972/73 tour of India and Pakistan, where he subsequently made his Test Match debut and proved to be a very capable England leader.

However, the writing was on the wall as far as the Glamorgan side was concerned, and I lent my support to the committee's decision to replace him as captain for 1973. I still believe that this decision was correct, but the subsequent choice of his successor was, with hindsight, one of the biggest mistakes in Glamorgan's history. Several names were considered and, in the end, the choice seemed a natural one. Majid Khan had graced the side with distinction since 1967 when he burst on the scene with the Pakistani tourists and pummelled a brace of sixes for his country in their game against Glamorgan at Swansea. No sooner had he returned to the St. Helen's pavilion than Wilf Wooller popped his head around the changing room door and offered Majid a playing contract with the Welsh county from 1968 onwards.

Majid duly followed his father up to Cambridge where he successfully led the Light Blues and by the time we were making our deliberations in the Glamorgan committee room, Majid had been appointed captain of Pakistan. Surely then he was an ideal choice, even for those patriotic types always yearning for an all-Welsh side.

The Glamorgan squad of 1975. Standing: G Armstrong, JW Solanky, JA Hopkins, GP Ellis, AL Jones, G Richards and T Cordle. Seated: RC Davis, EW Jones, MJ Khan, A Jones and MA Nash.

Some years previously the blond-haired Ossie Wheatley had come from Warwickshire to take over the Glamorgan side, and had done it so successfully that he conquered the doubters to such an extent that they took him to their bosoms, and conjured up the nickname "Dai Peroxide". Majid, too, was universally accepted, and it was felt that, by his own standards, he would have the loyalty of every *player on the staff. In addition, it was felt that giving him the reins of power would strengthen his interest in the development of the youngsters under his control; that he would, both on and off the field, be an inspiration and an example to the Welsh novices.*

Sadly, it did not work out that way. Majid was no extrovert, and, after he had batted and was back in the pavilion, more often than not would retire into a corner of the dressing-room with a book until it was time to take to the field again. On such occasions, when the opponents batted, he would remain unobtrusive, standing at first slip, except when the weather was cold, when he would draw attention to himself by standing with his hands in his pockets; which action, although doubtless done to keep his hands warm and assist his catching ability, nevertheless contrived to upset some of the spectators, who were given the impression that Majid was bored with the proceedings.

Furthermore, the various aspects of socialising after play and at other events were not for the likes of him. He did not drink alcohol, because of his religious beliefs, and, therefore, tended not to mix after play. During the luncheon interval on away grounds he would opt for a snack in the dressing-room rather than sit with the opposing captain and committee, and the empty chair on the top table sometimes was a source of embarrassment. Majid was not interested in supervising pre-match nets or tactical talks, or indeed in arriving early at the ground to advise the administration of the selected team in order that score cards could be printed, although he had insisted on having the last word as far as selection were concerned. In reality, it was just that Majid was interested in playing cricket only, and, once off the field, he withdrew into his normal unobtrusive shell, not seeking or liking publicity, or being in the spotlight normally accepted by sporting heroes.

Once more, the morale of the side was affected, and, once more, a committee decision was in the offing. The outcome was as expected. Majid was deposed, but unfortunately, in a rather tactlessly way. Wilf Wooller, as secretary of the Club, had long been aware of Majid's failings as a captain, and, in his own way, he took him to task about the matter. More than that, he began to visit the dressing-room and nets, seeking to improve the position of a deteriorating side by trying to impart his knowledge of the game to all and sundry. However, Wilf's tendency to browbeat and berate was foreign to Majid's own methods, and animosity quickly developed, which ultimately killed any forlorn hope that, after being deposed, Majid would continue to serve Glamorgan in his former capacity of their leading batsman.

It was a very sad time in the affairs of Glamorgan CCC, and brought benefit to no one, but, for the second time in a few years, I had no hesitation in supporting the committee decision to seek yet another captain. The new choice again seemed logical and inevitable, as the vice-captain and senior professional was Alan Jones, one of the greatest Glamorgan players since Emrys Davies, and also one of the nicest persons imaginable.

A true Welshman, loved and respected by all, Alan was the next and obvious choice. As expected, he was delighted to accept the position, and carried out his duties with his usual decorum – quietly and efficiently. However, there are many occasions when the captain needs to be capable of delivering an explosive verbal rocket to a player not giving his all, or one guilty of a misdemeanour, and be immune to the fact that it would tend to make him unpopular, at least to the recipient, in my mind, of his outburst until the effect wore off. Alan Jones, like Johnnie Clay before him, was too gentle a person to take this kind of action, which was unfortunate, because certain senior players in the side took advantage of his leniency, and did not always pull their weight. The inevitable happened. Playing results were poor, despite Alan leading Glamorgan to their first-ever Cup Final at Lord's when they met Middlesex in the final of the 1977 Gillette Cup.

Things did not pick up in 1978; the Club's members had become both despondent and critical, and the committee were obliged to take yet another decision. It was felt that Alan should be allowed to revert back to his former position of vice-captain and senior professional, and thus have no pressures to disturb him in what surely would be the last few years of his long and marvellous service to the Club.

The cricket committee deliberated at length on the subject of a successor; the one unanimous decision was that the next captain needed to be someone from outside the circle of the present senior players; someone worthy of a place in the team, and with the ability to direct, drive, and motivate the rest of the players. Three or four names were bandied about, and, in the end, the decision was made to engage Robin Hobbs. He had been an England player; had served Essex with distinction for many years, and, although the last few seasons had been spent in the comparative obscurity of

Minor Counties cricket with Suffolk, Robin was prepared to accept what we all knew would be a stern challenge. It was not a successful choice, and he soon went the way of his predecessors.

The net result was that during the 1970s and 1980s, Glamorgan members and supporters had to endure season after season of poor playing performances, when the will to win was far from evident; when lack-lustre batting, bowling and fielding made watching games an unhappy experience; when the so-called up-and-coming youngsters who had been brought to first-team level mainly through the coaching efforts of Phil Clift failed to grasp their opportunities; when their lack of application or concentration (or both) resulted in a string of mediocre scores with the bat; the loss of line and length when bowling, and dropped catches in the field.

Robin Hobbs

The subsequent appointment of Tom Cartwright as coach

and manager in 1978 was another cricket committee gamble made in an effort to put Glamorgan back on the cricketing map where they surely belonged. But even this did not work out as Tom only worked for a couple of seasons with the county club during which he didn't always see eye to eye with some of the players in his charge and subsequently, secured a post with the Welsh Cricket Association as national coach.

It is no secret that success on the field brings increased interest and support from the public; conversely, the lack of success brings not only a general lessening of interest and support but also much criticism of players and committee, much of it of a carping nature. The media, too, very often can (and will) add fuel to the fiery words of criticism by sensationalist reporting. In this respect, however, Glamorgan had every reason to be grateful to their ever-faithful local scribes, in particular those representing the "Western Mail" and "South Wales Echo", for the fair way in which matches were reported; the tendency to

Tom Cartwright

emphasise the good points, and the mild rebukes that came in the form of constructive criticism. The players knew their faults and limitations; the committee was aware of them, and the important need to introduce new blood.

On the plus side, the influx of overseas cricketers into the various county sides certainly proved to be beneficial. The quality of their play and their personalities, have brought back the spectators in their thousands, and, in their own teams, young players on the verge of establishing themselves gained in knowledge and confidence by being on the same field as these great men, and by being in their company from crease to dressing-room. Barry Richards, Clive Lloyd, Viv Richards, Mike Procter and dozens of later imports all helped to boost the finances of their counties by their very presence and by their performances.

Glamorgan have had their fair share of overseas players – some outstanding, some good, and a few who proved, for a variety of reasons, to be not-so-good. One of the first to come, and probably the best, apart from Viv Richards and Waqar Younis, was Bryan Davis, the West Indian top-order batsman. He quickly learned to adapt himself to the slower, lower bounce wickets of Wales; he produced many fine innings; he caught many catches at slip, and generally enhanced the morale of the side by his very pleasant disposition. It was unfortunate that he was unable to stay, but greater security came his way with an offer of permanent employment in the West Indies. We were sorry to lose him, but wished him well.

Roy Fredericks, the hard-hitting West Indies opening batsman was the next to come to Wales in the early 1970s, and he soon showed supporters his entertainment value with a series of fast scoring innings. In addition, he was no mean performer with the ball, and his teasing mixture of left-arm leg-breaks and googlies earned him

Roy Fredericks and Alan Jones.

many a wicket. Roy was another fine team man, full of fun, and easily fitted into the social as well as the cricketing activities. The pity was that he was not content to bide his time on the English wickets when the new ball was being swung and moving off the seam. He still went for his shots, and frequently holed out behind the wicket or at long-leg when hooking at short balls. Thus his tremendous potential was not realised, and his resulting inconsistency, certainly over-emphasised by Wilf Wooller, led to his not being invited to accept a new contract. In hindsight, this decision was utterly wrong, as, with a little more careful handling, surely he would have had the good sense to adapt his game to our conditions.

With the departure of Roy Fredericks, the general consensus of opinion was that Glamorgan's desperate need was for a really quick bowler, and, when our West Indies contact man reported that one Gregory Armstrong was highly recommended by such famous ex-players as Wes Hall and Jeff Stollmeyer, we quickly signed him. Gregory proved to be a very pleasant individual, willing and eager to learn how best to bowl on our wickets, and there was no doubt about it – he was a quickie! Unfortunately, one serious fault emerged; one which was never rectified. Gregory could not run up to the wicket and deliver the ball from the correct spot; he no-balled continuously and unmercifully. He tried ten-yard runs, twenty-yard runs, thirty-yard runs, but all to no avail. He would overstep, and be called. He sought advice from everyone; our coaches and senior players spent hours in the nets with him, but it was no good, and he had to go.

The next one to come on the scene was also a West Indian. It seemed that we were pinning our faith in the West Indies' ability to produce someone who at last would provide us with what we wanted – a consistent world-class match-winner. With

Collis King, in 1977, we found that we had a genuine all-rounder who was determined to pull his weight and give of his best. His reputation as a hard-hitting batsman and more than useful change bowler was justified, and there were occasions during the season when he electrified players and spectators alike by his marvellous eye and tremendous range of powerful shots.

Although he always gave one hundred per cent to the team and his captain, Collis also tended to be rather impetuous – much like Roy Fredericks – and too often gave his wicket away. At the very time when he had an opportunity of proving his worth, in the Gillette Cup Final against Middlesex in 1977, he had a bad match, not only failing with the bat and ball, but dropping a vital catch in the slips, which, had he held it, may have altered the whole course of the match. In the

Rodney Ontong

event, the Packer business came to a head; Collis was one of those put under contract to him, and he was not considered to be available for the Glamorgan playing staff in 1978 and we parted company with him.

One young player from South Africa who joined the staff after initial coaching at Lord's was Rodney Ontong who showed great promise as an all-rounder, and developed really well after being given a chance to bat at number three. The unfortunate part was that, despite having spent several years in this country, he just missed the eligible qualifying period that would have considered him to be a non-overseas player.

Some though were not so keen on the overseas contingent, believing that they sought and obtained far better financial terms than their British counterparts; that they hawked their services around, creating a form of Dutch auction until they got what they wanted; that they stifled the growth potential of young cricketers from this country by denying them a possible place in the side, a place which would probably have been available if the overseas player were not on the scene.

Most of those with differing views, however, generally agreed that the main danger was to have too many overseas signings in any one county side, and the Test and

County Cricket Board (now the ECB) were aware of the situation, and looked into the matter very carefully. As a one time member of the registration sub-committee at Lord's, I attended a series of meetings – and it was interesting to listen to both sides of the argument. The eventual outcome from these discussions was a decision to restrict each county to just one overseas player.

By the late 1980s, I had spent nearly twenty years in the labour of love that is a committee man and I eventually decided that it was time someone younger took over, and accordingly, stepped down. My link with Glamorgan had almost topped the fifty-year mark, and the fact that the committee saw fit to make me an Honorary Life Member of the Club meant that I shall never entirely sever my connection with either Glamorgan CCC or those many friends whose company I have enjoyed during that period.

From a position in recent years on the back benches, I have watched Glamorgan CCC develop a new headquarters and Test Match stadium. The plush new facilities are a far cry from what I first experienced when a schoolboy watching at the Arms Park during the 1930s and as a junior professional during the late 1940s. It is certainly a sign of progress and, I sincerely hope as well, a sign of financial stability and security. I know that the latter are difficult to achieve in uncertain financial times but I applaud the club for what they have done and I will continue to follow their fortunes.

20

MARRIAGE, FAMILY AND LATER YEARS

This book has so far focussed on Jim's life – as a sportsman, professional cricketer, businessman and latterly as a committee member. But just like batting or bowling, it involves a partnership, as well as others playing a supporting role. Jim's rich – and lucky – life would not have been so enjoyable or successful had he not had the support and strength of his family, so this closing chapter, once again in Jim's own words, pays tribute to the others in "Team Jim."

It really is remarkable that, where professional sportsmen are concerned, it is possible to lead a happily married life despite the long periods that you are away from home, and all despite the many temptations that are met throughout their travels. Professional cricketers today (and in my day), in addition to being away from home for most of the summer, are often separated from their wives and families for most of the winter months. If they are good enough, they may well join an England party on tour abroad; they may take part in shorter sponsored private tours abroad, or they may accept many of the winter coaching engagements available in Australia or South Africa. In all cases, they are able to earn money while soaking up the sun, which must be a far better proposition than braving the cold winters at home, and looking for part-time work, which is hard to come by.

There must be many marriages that can't stand the strain of such long partings, and for those that do, a break-up can often result from boredom on the part of the wife, left on her own for long periods, with the attendant frustrations of trying to cope with the non-stop requirements of a growing family.

I have been one of the lucky ones. Admittedly, I did not indulge in winter activities abroad, preferring to take my chance with part-time employment in this country, and to remain with my wife and family. As a result, I have seen my two sons and daughter grow to maturity in a reasonably sane and healthy manner whilst my marriage survived the passage of time, despite my wife having to contend with my many different moods and the odd traits in my character.

Our initial meeting and subsequent courtship tended to confirm the contention that

Jim's parents celebrate their Golden Wedding Anniversary in 1972.

opposites attract. It happened in that golden year for Glamorgan, the Championship winning year of 1948. As a member of that side I, in common with the rest of the players, was in the public eye, and much in demand for autographs and personal attendances at both private and public functions. It was obvious that I should be a position to meet many eligible and attractive females, in particular those who idolised sporting personalities and followed them around. However, there was no one in that group who appealed to me.

Instead, the fateful meeting proved to have nothing to do with cricket. A non-cricketing school friend and I, just by chance, decided to visit the sea-side dance hall at Barry Island, a few miles from Cardiff, on a Saturday evening. We went early, before the place had warmed up, and seeing three girls sitting together at a table, I plucked up courage, walked over to them, and asked if one of them would like to dance. My wife swears that the other two pushed her up on to her feet, but she accepted the invitation, and a pleasant evening resulted. I liked the look of her and we arranged to meet on the following Tuesday. However, she did not turn up, apparently because she didn't want to, and that seemed to be the end of it. It wasn't, though, because, again by chance, my friend and I decided to visit the same dance hall the next Saturday evening, and there she was, also by chance. It seems that the girls, waiting at their local bus stop near the railway station just outside Penarth, decided to go to Cardiff if the bus came first. If, however, the train was first to come, they would go to the same seaside venue as before. The train came first, and we met again. This time, the impression I made must have been better, as Theresa Mary Margaret Amelia condescended to turn up for the next date, and so began our lasting and loving relationship.

Opposites attract, indeed. One of us was home loving, house proud, placid, considerate, sophisticated, and not particularly interested in sport. The other proved to be anything but! For all that, it is an established fact that when two people spend a life-time together, the characteristics of one tend to rub off on the other, and vice versa. I, too, have become a little house proud, and do not grumble when it is necessary to wash dishes, decorate, paint, and tend the garden. My wife, if short changed or sold shoddy goods while shopping, will demand rectification, and ensure that she gets it, which is something she would never have contemplated in the early days of marriage. In addition, she has been known to sit through a televised soccer match, and has even attended cricket and golf matches with me.

If there were one area in which our marriage could have broken down it would have been that of religion. I had always been brought up as a staunch Church of England worshipper, which is understandable when one considers that my father spent many years of his life as a church organist and choirmaster both in Cardiff and in the nearby village of St Fagans. In his later years he was also strongly involved with the famous Llandaff Cathedral along with my mother who was also devout in her beliefs. Since my early days as a chorister my own interest in of the church tended to wane, and virtually ceased altogether after my years of Army service. Ostensibly, it was because of compulsory church parades, which I was most unhappy to experience, but, in reality, those merely accelerated my lack of interest. It seemed to me that many people went to church just for the social contacts, and it astonished me to see some of the so-called sanctimonious regular attenders ridicule, demean, and gossip about other people, and generally act in a very unchristian like manner. I became very disenchanted with it all.

Naturally, when my engagement was announced, my parents were extremely concerned, because my wife-to-be was a practising Roman Catholic, and they were at pains to point out to me the likely problems arising from a mixed marriage, not the least being the up-bringing of any children. I was happy, because I believed that if both sides bent a little towards each other's ways, and made due allowances for each other's differences, the marriage would prosper. Two things confirmed my belief that my partner-to-be would try and meet me halfway: Soon after I met her, I told her that, if we were to go through life together, she could forget the Theresa Mary Margaret Amelia, as I intended to call her Terry, and so it became without quibble on her part. The second example came when I was off on one of my cricket tours, and she wrote me a couple of letters. On my return, I offered her my first present,

Jim (left) and Terry (right) socialising with friends.

and she unwrapped the parcel excitedly, to find – a dictionary! The moment she put it in her bag, instead of throwing it at me, I knew we should have no worries.

However, there were certain problems to overcome. As we were marrying in a Catholic church, out of deference to her mother's wishes, it was necessary for me to undergo three months' instruction from the Catholic priest. At first, he tried hard to convert me to the faith, but, in the end, realised that he had no chance, as I could be rather stubborn when anyone tried to tell me that I should be doing something different from my own inclination. He did, however, start to sow the seeds of doubt about the liaison with my wife-to-be, because, on one occasion, he had the gall to say to her: "Couldn't you find someone better than him?" – implying that any Catholic boy would have been preferable.

Anyway, the marriage went ahead, and we survived it all. When the first two children came, I made my own concessions, and they were brought up in the Catholic faith. In the end, though, the dangers of trying to thrust religion down the throats of others became apparent. My wife, who had been contributing regularly to the church for several years, the funds being earmarked for the building of a new church in the locality, was horrified to discover that, ultimately, the money had been used for an entirely different project, without so much as by your leave. It was the beginning of a waning interest on her part, so much so that, as the children grew older, she advised them to go their own way in religious matters if they so desired, and when the third child came along, he was brought up as a non-Catholic.

Our two sons are not practising church goers, but my daughter, who has been one of the two brought up as a Catholic, has become a regular worshiper at a Church of England establishment; encourages her own daughter to attend there, and takes a great interest in the ancillary social activities. The whole going to prove that life's little complexities tend to sort themselves out if they are given the chance.

During the 1980s, our bi-annual visits to the apartment in Mallorca ceased. There were a couple of reasons. The advent of much building work in the vicinity meant that the peaceful environment was being disturbed too much for our liking. It was a habit with the locals who had ambitions to own property to save their money, and, when they had sufficient, to purchase a plot of land. Then, a little more saving, and they would start to build the foundations. Similar saving would enable them in time to construct the ground floor, first floor, and the roof, followed by occupation. This very often took many months before completion, so the noise, and the mess were on-going. A second factor was that, in the apartment above us, were a retired English couple, with whom we did not see eye-to-eye. The friction began with the noise of her shoes on the floor above our flat. As the floors consisted of a hard marble like compound, the clumping from one spot to another proved to be very distracting, and a quiet word from us did not have the desired effect. The net result was that, using the modern description we encountered the "neighbours from hell".

Anyway, the decision was made, and we disposed of our assets, and moved permanently back to the UK. There was one advantage – now we were no longer tied to spending our holiday time in one place. The world was our oyster. Consequently, over the next few years we travelled to the United States twice; Egypt and the Nile; Malta and Madeira. We also decided, after a break of some ten years, to visit Mallorca just to see if things had changed. We acquired a farm bungalow near Pollensa in the North of the island, and thoroughly enjoyed our two weeks. One day was spent in our former haunt of Porto Cristo, and we were astounded at the change from a small fishing port to a tourist trap full of fast food restaurants, bars and the like. We did not stay!

Malta and Madeira were much the same as other resorts; sun, sand and airport delays, but the trips to the US were exhilarating. The first was to Orlando and Disney World, where, quite naturally, we took our ten-year old grand-daughter, and she had a great time. The second week of that sojourn was spent on the Gulf coast, and we were able to relax after the many attractions of the Orlando area.

The other United States trip was booked with Saga, who cater for the older ones, and took in a coach journey on the West coast. We flew to San Francisco, had two days to unwind and visit such well-known spots as Alcatraz and the Golden Gate Bridge; joined our coach party, and travelled from there to Yosemite National Pak, Las Vegas, Boulder Dam, the Grand Canyon, San Diego, and back to Los Angeles for our flight home. Although it meant virtually living in and out of a suit case, what with the packing and unpacking, it was well worth it.

Although, to all intents and purposes, I had retired from business in my middle fifties, I was not going to be allowed to stagnate – far from it. A friend of mine who owned a chemical company had need of a credit controller for a couple of days each week, and asked me to do it for him. Well, I thought it would keep me out of mischief, and out of my wife's way, and so it proved. However, I became more and more involved with the business and ultimately was asked if I would take over the duties of Company Secretary, doing a few hours each day. It was agreed, and I found it absorbing, reasonably lucrative as an addition to my old-age pension, and fulfilling. From that small beginning came more than fifteen years in that post, and it is only now that I have reached the pipe and slippers stage in life.

Not normally one to do things by halves, I decided to go the whole hog; to give up my work on various committees. The only activity I retained was that of Secretary of the Glamorgan Former Players Association, which involved the organisation of our reunion meeting once in each year.

It was really great during the 1990s and early 2000s to meet up with so many of my former colleagues once again and to swop tales about life on the county circuit.

Jim at a former players reunion at Sophia Gardens with George Clements, Allan Watkins and Jeff Jones.

The number of stalwarts from the 1930s and 1940s steadily decreased over time, and as each year went by, and the roll call was read out at our annual gatherings, I found myself extremely lucky to still be enjoying generally good heaslth and an ability to still to get to matches under my own steam. I have been very lucky to have achieved what I have in business, sport and in family life, and I continue to be most fortunate. Long may that continue!